Vocabulary Ladders
Understanding Word Nuances

disgusting
inedible
bland
scrumptious
succulent

Authors

Timothy Rasinski, Ph.D.

Melissa Cheesman Smith, M.Ed.

SHELL EDUCATION

Publishing Credits

Robin Erickson, *Production Director*; Lee Aucoin, *Creative Director*;
Timothy J. Bradley, *Illustration Manager*; Emily R. Smith, M.A.Ed., *Editorial Director*;
Jennifer Wilson, *Editor*; Amber Goff, *Editorial Assistant*; Danielle Nelson, *Editorial Assistant*;
Grace Alba Le, *Designer*; Corinne Burton, M.A.Ed., *Publisher*

Image Credits

All images Shutterstock

Standards

© 2007 Teachers of English to Speakers of Other Languages, Inc. (TESOL)
© 2007 Board of Regents of the University of Wisconsin System. World-Class Instructional Design and Assessment (WIDA)
© Copyright 2010. National Governors Association Center for Best Practices and Council of Chief State School Officers. All rights reserved.

Shell Education

5301 Oceanus Drive
Huntington Beach, CA 92649-1030
http://www.shelleducation.com
ISBN 978-1-4258-1305-5
© 2014 Shell Educational Publishing, Inc.

Table of Contents

Table of Contents *(cont.)*

A Note to the Educator

"The difference between the right word and the almost right word
is the difference between lightning and a lightning bug."

—Mark Twain, *The Wit and Wisdom of Mark Twain*

Choosing the right word adds power and richness to a writer's message. Understanding the reason for that choice adds precision and depth to the reader's comprehension. This book provides a unique approach to vocabulary study that supports both writers and readers and offers several advantages. First, it sharpens students' thinking and refines their sense of the underlying concept. Second, it encourages students to consider the purposes and circumstances for selecting specific words so they are used effectively. Third, it provides the writer or speaker with a range of words from which to choose to most appropriately express the meaning he or she intends to convey.

The activities in this book include instructional concepts from the research on vocabulary teaching and learning. The activities require students to review and clarify specific word meanings and relate them to appropriate situations. Students will also have the opportunity to solidify their learning by applying word meanings to their personal experiences.

While the materials in these books are tightly organized, and the activities are clear and straightforward, the connections among words often are not. Word relationships are complex, and there may be several reasonable interpretations of how words should be arranged along a continuum. The word orders in the ladders are not cast in stone. Many times the differences among word meanings are less a matter of degree and more one of the context or situation. To be most effective in increasing the breadth and depth of student vocabularies, teachers must encourage students to explain their own understandings of the word meanings and explain how they are connected and how they may be used, and they must respect these explanations. It is in the process of talking about words that learning about them is best advanced. Thus, the ladders should not be seen as end points to be memorized, but as starting points for discussion, debate, and discovery.

—Jerry Zutell
Professor Emeritus
The Ohio State University

Research

> "Give me the right word and the right accent, and I will move the world."
>
> —Joseph Conrad

It is well established that success in reading requires readers to understand the individual words they encounter in text (Anderson and Freebody 1981; 1983; Becker 1977; Davis 1944; National Reading Panel 2000). Without the understanding of key words, it is very unlikely that readers will have a good understanding of the larger texts in which the words are embedded. Similarly, proficiency in writing requires writers to have a large array of words at their disposal. Word choice is consistently viewed as an important factor when judging the quality of a student's writing. Indeed, the Common Core State Standards that are now guiding instruction in schools across the United States have identified vocabulary acquisition as critical to success not only in literacy but also in learning within the content areas.

Vocabulary instruction is crucial to success in learning to read and write in English. But developing students' vocabularies has been challenging for teachers over the years. One reason is that English contains more words than nearly any other language. That means that teachers not only have a lot of words to teach but also need to be very selective in the words they choose. It is not very productive to teach words that students will rarely encounter in oral and written language. Yet in many vocabulary programs, this is exactly the approach taken—teach students unusual and rare words that they are unlikely to hear in speech or read in print.

In classrooms around the country, we see well-meaning and hardworking teachers who teach vocabulary as a list of weekly words, often paired with a reading anthology. Students are expected to find and memorize the dictionary definitions of the words for a test at the end of the week. The following week, the routine begins again with a new set of words. Many students do not like word study, and we understand why. Rote memorization of definitions of unusual and rare words for which students have little use or exposure to is likely to shut down almost anyone's interest in words, as it is a chore rather than an exciting enterprise.

There are many tools available for exploring and expanding vocabulary. One of the best is the tried-and-true thesaurus. Most writers carry thesauri with them so that when they need just the right word to express a meaning, they can find it from an array of semantically related words. Yet in our visits to classrooms across the country, we find that the set of thesauri found in most classrooms goes untouched. Many teachers are not familiar with and have not been taught ways to use a thesaurus as an ally to their instruction. This book addresses that problem by providing an engaging approach to the study of semantically related words.

Research *(cont.)*

Effective Vocabulary Instruction

Although there is no single scientifically endorsed way to teach vocabulary to all students, there are central principles that can guide teachers in creating effective instruction (Brabham et al. 2012; Nagy 1988; Stahl 1986). These principles are:

1. **Meaningful Clusters**—Organize words into meaningful clusters in which the words to be taught are related in some useful way. Words can be clustered by relation to theme or topic (*volcano, lava, magma*), word derivation (*bicycle, bifocals, biannual*), or essential meaning (*big, large, enormous*). Since words in a cluster are related, students can make connections among words within each cluster.

2. **Meaningful Use**—Have students engage in meaningful use of the words by exploring the words in multiple reading and writing activities.

3. **Repeated Encounters**—To learn words deeply, students need to encounter the words repeatedly in various texts and practice using them in oral and written language.

Throughout the years, we have used these three principles and have found them to be quite successful. We have added our own two principles to make vocabulary instruction even more successful. These principles include:

4. **Regular and Consistent Routine**—Vocabulary instruction should follow a regular and consistent routine so that students are well aware of the procedures for word learning, and their time is spent in exploring words rather than learning new procedures.

5. **Brief Instruction**—Formal vocabulary instruction should be brief. In order to provide adequate instruction in all required areas, time is of the essence. Formal vocabulary instruction, then, should take approximately 15 minutes per day. Keep in mind, however, that time may also be devoted to the study of word decoding and spelling in addition to vocabulary. Also, we feel that informal vocabulary instruction and learning can and should take place throughout the school day—during reading and writing as well as in content-area instruction.

We have attempted to incorporate these fundamental principles into a novel approach to vocabulary instruction called *Vocabulary Ladders*.

Research *(cont.)*

What Are Vocabulary Ladders?

Vocabulary Ladders (VL) is a cluster approach to teaching many words at once. The words in a VL are semantically or meaningfully related to one another (much like in a thesaurus). Unlike many vocabulary lists, we have included many words that students are already familiar with so that the focus of each lesson is not on learning a large number of new vocabulary words but understanding the nuances of the words they may have already encountered. Think of the words that you might find in an entry of a thesaurus. All of the words have similar essential meanings. However, they may all differ in degree (*miniscule* vs. *small*) or nuance (*cute* vs. *beautiful*). The skill of determining nuance in words is a key component to the new Common Core State Standards. So not only can the words within a semantic cluster be grouped together but they can also be organized according to their degree of essential meaning or level of nuance. These connections can also merge into opposite meanings at the other end of the spectrum. Through this approach, students not only learn groups of related words but they also are given opportunities to explore the shades of meaning that exist within each cluster. Ten minutes of VL instruction three to four days a week leads to deepening students' understanding of words they may be familiar with and expanding the sheer size of their vocabularies. Regular work with VL will help students understand and use the relative degree of meaningful difference between words in an engaging way. Below are two examples of vocabulary ladders that we have used in our instruction with students:

> The skill of determining nuance in words is a key component to the new Common Core State Standards.

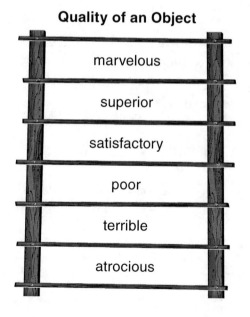

Temperature

- boiling
- hot
- warm
- chilly
- freezing

Quality of an Object

- marvelous
- superior
- satisfactory
- poor
- terrible
- atrocious

Research *(cont.)*

As you can see, the words in each cluster are related by their essential or base meaning or theme, but they also differ from one another in the magnitude of their essential meanings. Exploring words in this way will help students see that authors have large palettes of words to choose from when writing. A writer can choose just the right word to express his or her meaning. Knowing these words will help increase students' understanding when they read what authors have written. At the same time, studying VL will expand students' vocabulary palettes so that when they write, they can also choose precise words that exactly fit the meaning and nuance that they are trying to express (e.g., *Barbara felt sad as she left home* vs. *Barbara felt teary as she left home*). Certainly, teachers can create VL themselves to use with students. However, teachers today are so busy with all their instructional and administrative duties that it is difficult for them to create student word lists to use on a consistent (weekly) basis for students. We have done the legwork for teachers by creating a complete set of VL that they can use with their students. With the VL in hand, teachers can now engage students regularly in exploring clusters of semantically related words. As a result, vocabulary knowledge will increase and students' reading comprehension and writing composition will improve.

Vocabulary knowledge is essential to school success—in reading, writing, and learning in all content areas. Knowledge of words allows the learning of new text to occur more easily, especially when students independently encounter complex text or close readings. Although there is no single way to teach students vocabulary, we feel *Vocabulary Ladders: Understanding Word Nuances* provides you—the teacher—and your students with a productive and engaging way to explore and discover the words that may allow your students to be successful.

Implementing Vocabulary Ladders in the Classroom

Recognizing the time limits of teachers and students, we developed the VL approach to take no more than 10 to 15 minutes, three to four days a week. In these short, powerful lessons, students will be immersed in the exploration of word clusters of related words through teacher-selected activities. Students will be asked to explore the words, put the words into a meaningful order, use the words in constructing sentences, and use the words in written compositions. Through this process, students will learn the cluster of words in depth, embed the meanings into their permanent oral vocabularies, use the words to help them understand the texts they read, and improve their writing proficiency and accuracy.

This book is made up of 20 lessons. An additional six lessons as well as a blank *Activity Cards* template can be found on the Digital Resource CD (filenames: additionallessons.pdf; cardstemplate.pdf). Each lesson contains a theme and a cluster of words that will be explored over several days. On the next page is the general plan used in VL for teaching nuanced meanings of word clusters. This daily breakdown is just a suggestion. We encourage teachers to decide what flow works best for their students. As the teacher, you are free to implement each weekly lesson however you like. Each lesson can be done over three, four, or five days. We do recommend that at least three days per week are devoted to vocabulary ladders. Massing the weekly activities into one or two days will not provide the rich, in-depth coverage of the words that will allow for deep learning and continuous use.

Note: We recommend that you allow students to work in groups on Day 1. The discussion that occurs within the groups as they attempt to organize the words is quite valuable and likely critical to cementing these words in their permanent oral vocabularies. Those students who have a more thorough understanding of the words will assist students who may not be as familiar with them. Discussing and exploring word relationships is more valuable than establishing a single correct order, so argument and debate are encouraged. (Each lesson provides a reasonably correct order that can be used in the follow-up activities.) The key is to become acquainted with the words, discuss the words, and explore how the words might be ordered.

The following page provides a suggested schedule for implementing each lesson. By the final day of the lesson, students will have expanded vocabularies and will have deeper understandings of the nuances or shades of meaning embedded in the cluster of words. By this time, students have either referenced, orally stated/defined, or used the words in context multiple times. Through multiple experiences, the words will become part of their personal vocabulary banks.

Implementing Vocabulary Ladders in the Classroom *(cont.)*

Day 1 | **Introduce and Discuss Words**

On Day 1, students will:

- review the words in the specified cluster and identify the theme that connects them (e.g., *colossal*, *huge*, *itty-bitty* all relate to *size*).
- work in groups to identify and discuss a reasonably correct order based on the meanings of the words.

For detailed information on the **Activity Cards** and **Vocabulary Ladders** activity sheets that will be used on this day, see page 15.

Day 2 | **Order Words**

On Day 2, students will:

- order the words how they think they should be ordered.
- work in groups to explain why words are ordered the way they are.

For detailed information on the **Ordering Words** activity sheet that will be used on this day, see page 16.

Day 3 | **Use Words in Context**

On Day 3, students will:

- carefully choose words from the cluster based on context to complete sentences.
- complete sentence stems by providing explanations that relate to targeted words.

For detailed information on the **Sentence Clues** and **Sentence Stems** activity sheets that will be used on this day, see pages 17–18.

Day 4 | **Use Words in Writing**

On Day 4, students will:

- write responses to a prompt using various words from the theme.
- share their writings with partners.

For detailed information on the **Write About It!** activity sheet that will be used on this day, see page 19.

Implementing Vocabulary Ladders in the Classroom *(cont.)*

Tips for Extensions

■ Post words for the week in (and out of) the classroom on charts or posters, and encourage students to use them in their conversation and writing.

■ Find ways to use the words of the week when communicating with students.

■ Create larger cards with the words on them to use in language centers where students can order (or sort) them in different ways such as number of syllables or negative or positive connotations.

■ Once students have a collection of 10 to 20 words from various lessons, have them sort the words along various dimensions. Students can be creative in coming up with their own ways to sort, or the teacher can provide the sorting topics such as sorting words into one-, two-, and three-syllables, sorting words that have more than one meaning and words that do not, and sorting words that have positive connotations and words that do not.

■ Students can create "mini-posters" of one of the words from the list, drawing a picture that specifically addresses the nuance of the word (mini-posters could also be added to language centers for students to try to match the word to the poster).

■ Encourage students to find (and celebrate) the words of the week in the books and other texts they are reading independently and during teacher read-alouds.

■ Incorporate the words in other word-study activities such as word games like WORDO. For information on how to play WORDO, including templates, see the Digital Resource CD (filename: wordo.pdf).

■ Encourage parents to use the words in their own interactions with their children. Send the words home for parents on a set of cards or paper; put the words on your classroom website home page so that parents have access to them.

■ As students work with the words in each vocabulary ladder, encourage them to think of other words that can be added. You may ask students to pose their additions in the following manner: *I think _____ fits on the ladder because it means _____. It should go between _____ and _____ because _____.*

■ Collect old paint samples that have the same number of shades as the words in the lesson. Have students write each word on a shade of paint and glue the sample in a notebook or word journal.

How to Use This Book

Lesson Overview

In each lesson's introductory page, information is offered to the teacher to help plan his or her implementation of the student activity pages. The following is addressed:

The **title** is a quick indicator of the theme of the lesson. With this, you may want to gather reading material or other resources that relate to the theme in order to further engage students with the vocabulary words.

The **objective** indicates the range of meaning students will be working with throughout the lesson.

A **materials list** identifies the components of the lesson.

A suggested **answer key** is provided for quick and easy reference. It provides either concrete answers, where applicable, or it suggests specific content for teachers to look out for.

Additional words that are associated with the theme are highlighted to further challenge students.

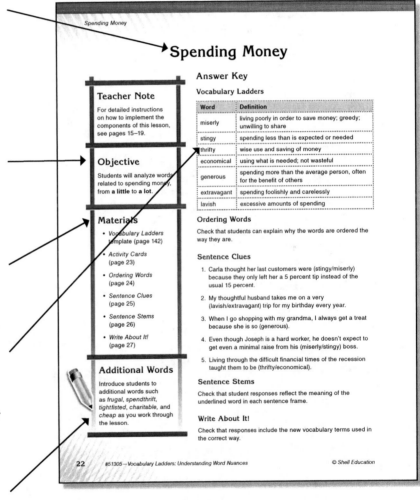

How to Use This Book *(cont.)*

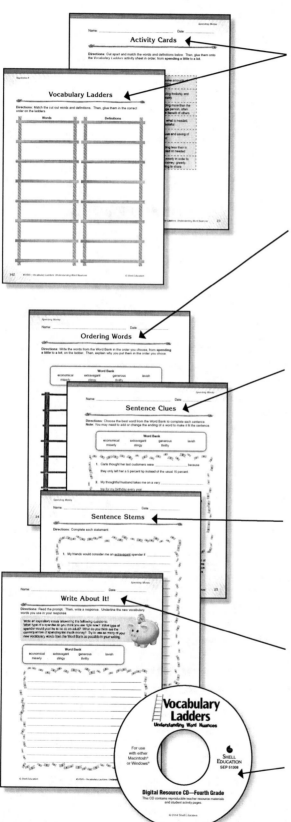

The words and definitions in each lesson are provided on **activity cards**. Students will cut these apart and glue them on the **Vocabulary Ladders** activity sheet. For detailed information on how to implement these activity sheets, see page 15.

With the **Ordering Words** activity, students write the words in an order of their choosing and then explain why they put the words in that order. For detailed information on how to implement this activity sheet, see page 16.

With the **Sentence Clues** activity, students choose the best word from their Vocabulary Ladders to complete sentences. For detailed information on how to implement this activity sheet, see page 17.

With the **Sentence Stems** activity, students respond to sentence frames that deal with the Vocabulary Ladders words. You may wish to have students write their responses and then share with partners, in a group, or in front of the class. For detailed information on how to implement this activity sheet, see page 18.

With the **Write About It!** activity, students read a prompt and use their themed vocabulary words in their responses. For detailed information on how to implement this activity sheet, see page 19.

All of the activity sheets and teacher resources can be found on the **Digital Resource CD**.

How to Use This Book (cont.)

How to Implement the Lessons

Vocabulary Ladders and Activity Cards

Objective

Students will match words with their definitions and put them in a meaningful order.

Procedures

1. Distribute the *Activity Cards* sheet found on the second page of each lesson.

2. Introduce the words in the left column. Explain that all of the words and definitions on the sheet have to do with a specific theme (e.g., *temperature*, *size*), but vary in level of meaning, or nuance. For example, the words *chilly* and *lukewarm* both deal with temperature, but they have different meanings. Discuss each word with students.

3. Have students cut the words and definitions apart. Caution them to be careful with cards after they are cut out so that they do not lose them. You may want to have the students write their initials on the backs of the cards.

4. Put students in small groups. Have them work together to match each word with its definition. Then, have each student within the group put the words in order based on meaning. Allow students to explain their thinking to their groups after they have ordered the words. Once all students have had opportunities to order the words and share, guide them toward the one reasonably correct way the words have been organized for the lesson.

5. Write the ordered words on the board, a vocabulary-ladder chart, or a word wall for students to revisit throughout the week.

6. Distribute the *Vocabulary Ladders* template found on page 142. Explain that students will use the ladder on the left to glue the words in nuance order beginning at the top of the ladder. Once all the words have been glued, have students glue the corresponding definitions on the ladder to the right.

7. You may wish to have students keep their *Vocabulary Ladders* to use with the remaining activity sheets in this lesson.

Optional Tips

■ You may wish to make multiple copies of the activity cards for students to place in personal vocabulary journals or to take home and review the vocabulary words with family members.

■ Copy the activity cards on colored paper so they are not easily lost once they are cut apart.

How to Use This Book (cont.)

How to Implement the Lessons (cont.)

Ordering Words

Objective

Students will write words in a meaningful order and explain important differences between the meanings of two of the words.

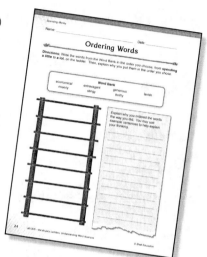

Procedures

1. Distribute the *Ordering Words* activity sheet found on the third page of each lesson.

2. Review the words in the Word Bank. You may wish to have volunteers read the definitions for each of the words from the *Vocabulary Ladders* activity sheet.

3. Instruct students to write the words from the Word Bank on the ladder in order of nuance that they choose. Explain that they may feel that some of the words should be ordered in a different way.

4. Model for students what is expected of them. For example, if two of the words are *slender* and *lanky*, you could model how to explain your reasoning for ordering them a certain way by saying, "If I am ordering words from *skinny* to *overweight*, I think that *lanky* would come before *slender* because *lanky* makes me think of someone whose bones are showing and *slender* seems a little more healthy, even though it still means a person has a thin body."

5. Have students explain important differences in meanings between the words in the box to the right of the ladder.

6. Allow students to compare their explanations with partners or small groups.

Optional Tips

- Have students work together so they can discuss why the words are ordered the way they are on the ladder.

- Provide time for students to think about the important differences between words before they write them down.

How to Use This Book *(cont.)*

How to Implement the Lessons *(cont.)*

Sentence Clues

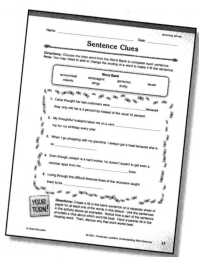

Objective

Students will use context and their knowledge of definitions to complete sentences with the most appropriate words.

Procedures

1. Distribute the *Sentence Clues* activity sheet found on the fourth page of each lesson.

2. Review the words from the *Vocabulary Ladders* activity sheet. Have volunteers read the definitions for all of the words to the class.

3. Explain to students that although there might be multiple answers, they should carefully review the definitions in order to provide what they feel is an appropriate response. Remind students that they may have to change the ending of a word to make it fit the sentence. Common endings include *-ed*, *-ing*, and *-ly*.

   Note: There are fewer sentences than words, though each word may be a reasonable answer to at least one of the sentences.

4. Have students compare their responses with partners. Then, allow for whole-class discussion.

5. Give students opportunities to construct their own sentence clues by completing the *Your Turn!* activity. Remind them to follow the directions on the activity sheet. Then, allow time for discussion.

Optional Tips

- Provide the additional vocabulary words to students for an added challenge and to use as possible answers.

- Have students work independently, in pairs, or in small groups depending on their skill levels.

How to Use This Book (cont.)

How to Implement the Lessons (cont.)

Sentence Stems

Objective

Students will respond to sentence stems using what they know about underlined targeted words.

Procedures

1. Distribute the *Sentence Stems* activity sheet found on the fifth page of each lesson.

2. Have students identify the underlined word in each sentence. Explain that they will have to write a response to finish each sentence making sure it relates to the meaning of the underlined word.

3. Once students have completed the activity sheet, have them share their responses with partners. Instruct them to explain how each response relates to the underlined word.

4. Invite small-group or whole-class discussion.

Optional Tips

- Have students work in groups to generate oral responses instead of writing them down.

- Have students create drawings that represent the meanings of their sentences.

- Allow students to act out their sentences in groups.

How to Use This Book (cont.)

How to Implement the Lessons (cont.)

Write About It!

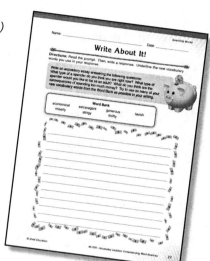

Objective

Students will respond to a writing prompt using the themed vocabulary.

Procedures

1. Distribute the *Write About It!* activity sheet found on the sixth page of each lesson.

2. Review the words from the *Vocabulary Ladders* activity sheet. Have volunteers read the definitions for all of the words to the class.

3. Have students read the prompt independently. Ask them what the prompt has to do with the theme.

4. Tell students to include at least two to three words from the Word Bank in their responses.

5. Provide time for students to write thoughtful responses. Instruct them to underline all of the new vocabulary words they use in their writing.

6. Have students read their papers to partners and discuss the similarities and differences between them.

Optional Tips

- Select volunteers to read their responses from an "author's chair." Have the rest of the class raise their hands as each vocabulary word is mentioned. Call on one student to explain why the word was an appropriate choice made by the author.

- Have students post their *Write About It!* activity sheets on a classroom bulletin board so that students can read the work of their classmates.

Correlation to the Standards

Shell Education is committed to producing educational materials that are research and standards based. In this effort, we have correlated all of our products to the academic standards of all 50 states, the District of Columbia, the Department of Defense Dependents Schools, and all Canadian provinces.

How to Find Standards Correlations

To print a customized correlation report of this product for your state, visit our website at http://www.shelleducation.com and follow the on-screen directions. If you require assistance in printing correlation reports, please contact our Customer Service department at 1-877-777-3450.

Purpose and Intent of Standards

Legislation mandates that all states adopt academic standards that identify the skills students will learn in kindergarten through grade twelve. Many states also have standards for Pre–K. This same legislation sets requirements to ensure the standards are detailed and comprehensive.

Standards are designed to focus instruction and guide adoption of curricula. Standards are statements that describe the criteria necessary for students to meet specific academic goals. They define the knowledge, skills, and content students should acquire at each level. Standards are also used to develop standardized tests to evaluate students' academic progress. Teachers are required to demonstrate how their lessons meet state standards. State standards are used in the development of all of our products, so educators can be assured they meet the academic requirements of each state.

Common Core State Standards

Many lessons in this book are aligned to the Common Core State Standards (CCSS). The standards support the objectives presented throughout the lessons and are provided on the Digital Resource CD (filename: standards.pdf).

TESOL and WIDA Standards

The lessons in this book promote English language development for English language learners. The standards listed on the Digital Resource CD (filename: standards.pdf) support the language objectives presented throughout the lessons.

Correlation to the Standards (cont.)

Standards Chart

Common Core State Standards	Lessons
Language.6.5—Demonstrate understanding of figurative language, word relationships, and nuances in word meaning	All Lessons
Language.6.5.b—Use the relationship between particular words (e.g., cause/effect, part/whole, item/category) to better understand each of the words	All Lessons
Language.6.5.c—Distinguish among the connotations (associations) of words with similar denotations (definitions) (e.g., *stingy, scrimping, economical, unwasteful, thrifty*)	All Lessons
TESOL/WIDA Standards	**Lessons**
English language learners **communicate** for **social**, **intercultural**, and **instructional** purposes within the school setting	All Lessons
English language learners **communicate** information, ideas, and concepts necessary for academic success in the area of **language arts**	All Lessons

Spending Money

Teacher Note

For detailed instructions on how to implement the components of this lesson, see pages 15–19.

Objective

Students will analyze words related to spending money, from **a little** to **a lot**.

Materials

- *Vocabulary Ladders* template (page 142)

- *Activity Cards* (page 23)

- *Ordering Words* (page 24)

- *Sentence Clues* (page 25)

- *Sentence Stems* (page 26)

- *Write About It!* (page 27)

Additional Words

Introduce students to additional words such as *frugal*, *spendthrift*, *tightfisted*, *charitable*, and *cheap* as you work through the lesson.

Answer Key

Vocabulary Ladders

Word	Definition
miserly	living poorly in order to save money; greedy; unwilling to share
stingy	spending less than is expected or needed
thrifty	wise use and saving of money
economical	using what is needed; not wasteful
generous	spending more than the average person, often for the benefit of others
extravagant	spending foolishly and carelessly
lavish	excessive amounts of spending

Ordering Words

Check that students can explain why the words are ordered the way they are.

Sentence Clues

1. Carla thought her last customers were (stingy/**miserly**) because they only left her a 5 percent tip instead of the usual 15 percent.

2. My thoughtful husband takes me on a very (**lavish**/extravagant) trip for my birthday every year.

3. When I go shopping with my grandma, I always get a treat because she is so (**generous**).

4. Even though Joseph is a hard worker, he doesn't expect to get even a minimal raise from his (miserly/**stingy**) boss.

5. Living through the difficult financial times of the recession taught them to be (**thrifty**/economical).

Sentence Stems

Check that student responses reflect the meaning of the underlined word in each sentence frame.

Write About It!

Check that responses include the new vocabulary terms used in the correct way.

Name: _____ Date: _____

Activity Cards

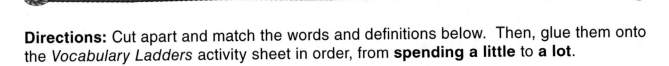

Directions: Cut apart and match the words and definitions below. Then, glue them onto the *Vocabulary Ladders* activity sheet in order, from **spending a little** to **a lot**.

economical	excessive amounts of spending
extravagant	spending foolishly and carelessly
generous	spending more than the average person, often for the benefit of others
lavish	using what is needed; not wasteful
miserly	wise use and saving of money
stingy	spending less than is expected or needed
thrifty	living poorly in order to save money; greedy; unwilling to share

Name: _____   Date: _____

Ordering Words

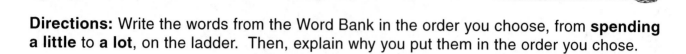

Directions: Write the words from the Word Bank in the order you choose, from **spending a little** to **a lot**, on the ladder. Then, explain why you put them in the order you chose.

Word Bank			
economical	extravagant	generous	lavish
miserly	stingy	thrifty	

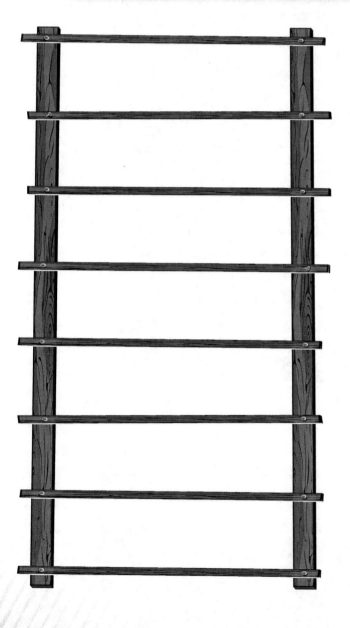

Explain why you ordered the words the way you did. You may use example sentences to help explain your thinking.

_____

_____

_____

_____

_____

_____

_____

_____

_____

_____

Name: _____ Date: _____

Sentence Clues

Directions: Choose the best word from the Word Bank to complete each sentence.
Note: You may need to add or change the ending of a word to make it fit the sentence.

Word Bank

economical	extravagant	generous	lavish
miserly	stingy	thrifty	

1. Carla thought her last customers were _____ because

   they only left her a 5 percent tip instead of the usual 15 percent.

2. My thoughtful husband takes me on a very _____

   trip for my birthday every year.

3. When I go shopping with my grandma, I always get a treat because she is

   so _____.

4. Even though Joseph is a hard worker, he doesn't expect to get even a

   minimal raise from his _____ boss.

5. Living through the difficult financial times of the recession taught

   them to be _____.

Directions: Create a fill-in-the-blank sentence on a separate sheet of
paper for at least one of the words in this lesson. Use the sentences
in the activity above as examples. Notice how a part of each sentence
provides a clue about which word fits best. Have a partner fill in the
missing word. Then, discuss why that word works best.

Name: _____   Date: _____

Sentence Stems

Directions: Complete each statement.

1. My friends would consider me an <u>extravagant</u> spender if _____

   _____

   _____ .

2. When I am feeling <u>generous</u>, I like to _____

   _____

   _____ .

3. I might become a <u>miserly</u> old man/woman if _____

   _____

   _____ .

4. I may have to learn to be more <u>economical</u> when _____

   _____

   _____ .

5. It is wise to be <u>thrifty</u> when buying a car because _____

   _____

   _____ .

Name: _____   Date: _____

Write About It!

Directions: Read the prompt. Then, write a response. Underline the new vocabulary words you use in your response.

Write an expository essay answering the following questions:
What type of a spender do you think you are right now? What type of spender would you like to be as an adult? What do you think are the consequences of spending too much money? Try to use as many of your new vocabulary words from the Word Bank as possible in your writing.

Word Bank			
economical	extravagant	generous	lavish
miserly	stingy	thrifty	

_____

_____

_____

_____

_____

_____

_____

_____

_____

_____

_____

_____

How Something Sounds: Loudness

Teacher Note

For detailed instructions on how to implement the components of this lesson, see pages 15–19.

Objective

Students will analyze words related to how something sounds, from **soft** to **loud**.

Materials

- *Vocabulary Ladders* template (page 142)
- *Activity Cards* (page 29)
- *Ordering Words* (page 30)
- *Sentence Clues* (page 31)
- *Sentence Stems* (page 32)
- *Write About It!* (page 33)

Additional Words

Introduce students to additional words such as *piercing*, *hushed*, *stifled*, and *bellowing* as you work through the lesson.

Answer Key

Vocabulary Ladders

Word	Definition
inaudible	impossible to be heard
muted	silent; not able to be heard
muffled	a faint sound that is hard to understand
audible	loud enough to be heard
boisterous	noisy and rowdy; exuberant
blaring	harsh and loud noise
deafening	extremely loud noise that could cause deafness if heard for a long time

Ordering Words

Check that students can explain why the words are ordered the way they are.

Sentence Clues

1. You could hear the (blaring/deafening) music from Bob's car even before you saw it coming around the corner.
2. The actor's voice was (inaudible) so I had to move closer to hear him at all.
3. The class next door was having a(n) (boisterous) party because they won the school contest.
4. The thick carpet (muffled/muted) the sound of her approaching footsteps.
5. The broken speaker system now made a(n) (audible) noise, so we knew it was working.

Sentence Stems

Check that student responses reflect the meaning of the underlined word in each sentence frame.

Write About It!

Check that responses include the new vocabulary terms used in the correct way.

Name: _____   Date: _____

Activity Cards

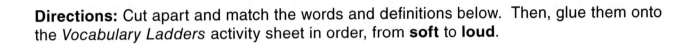

Directions: Cut apart and match the words and definitions below. Then, glue them onto the *Vocabulary Ladders* activity sheet in order, from **soft** to **loud**.

audible	extremely loud noise that could cause deafness if heard for a long time
blaring	harsh and loud noise
boisterous	noisy and rowdy; exuberant
deafening	loud enough to be heard
inaudible	a faint sound that is hard to understand
muffled	silent; not able to be heard
muted	impossible to be heard

Name: _____ Date: _____

Ordering Words

Directions: Write the words from the Word Bank in the order you choose, from **soft** to **loud**, on the ladder. Then, explain why you put them in the order you chose.

Word Bank

audible	blaring	boisterous	deafening
inaudible	muffled	muted	

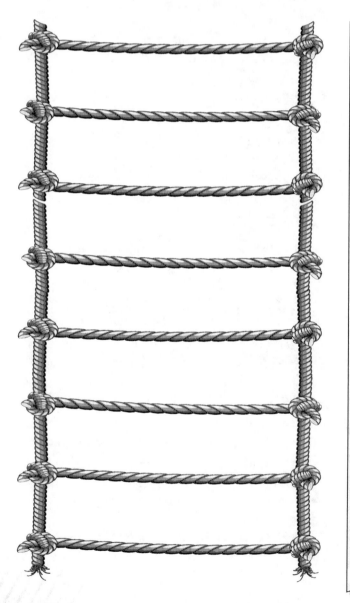

Explain why you ordered the words the way you did. You may use example sentences to help explain your thinking.

_____

_____

_____

_____

_____

_____

_____

_____

_____

_____

_____

Name: _____ Date: _____

Sentence Clues

Directions: Choose the best word from the Word Bank to complete each sentence.
Note: You may need to add or change the ending of a word to make it fit the sentence.

Word Bank

audible	blaring	boisterous	deafening
inaudible	muffled	muted	

---

1. You could hear the _____ music from Bob's car even before you saw it coming around the corner.

2. The actor's voice was _____ so I had to move closer to hear him at all.

3. The class next door was having a(n) _____ party because they won the school contest.

4. The thick carpet _____ the sound of her approaching footsteps.

5. The broken speaker system now made a(n) _____ noise, so we knew it was working.

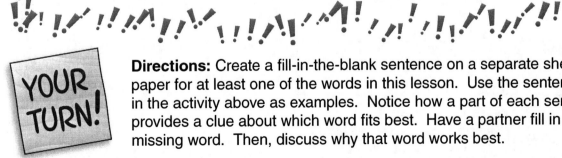

YOUR TURN!

Directions: Create a fill-in-the-blank sentence on a separate sheet of paper for at least one of the words in this lesson. Use the sentences in the activity above as examples. Notice how a part of each sentence provides a clue about which word fits best. Have a partner fill in the missing word. Then, discuss why that word works best.

Name: _____ Date: _____

Sentence Stems

Directions: Complete each statement.

1. I would <u>mute</u> the television if _____

   _____

   _____ .

2. Because the sound was <u>muffled</u>, I had to _____

   _____

   _____ .

3. I would become more <u>boisterous</u> if _____

   _____

   _____ .

4. My teacher's voice was barely <u>audible</u> so I had to _____

   _____

   _____ .

5. I would want my footsteps to be <u>inaudible</u> when _____

   _____

   _____ .

#51305—*Vocabulary Ladders: Understanding Word Nuances*   © Shell Education

Name: _____ Date: _____

Write About It!

Directions: Read the prompt. Then, write a response. Underline the new vocabulary words you use in your response.

Write a descriptive essay focusing on the sense of sound. You can describe a normal day in your life, a day at an amusement park, and so on. Try to use as many of your new vocabulary words from the Word Bank as possible in your writing.

Word Bank

audible	blaring	boisterous	deafening
inaudible	muffled	muted	

_____

_____

_____

_____

_____

_____

_____

_____

_____

_____

_____

Tastiness

Teacher Note

For detailed instructions on how to implement the components of this lesson, see pages 15–19.

Objective

Students will analyze words related to eating, from **gross** to **tasty**.

Materials

- *Vocabulary Ladders* template (page 142)
- *Activity Cards* (page 35)
- *Ordering Words* (page 36)
- *Sentence Clues* (page 37)
- *Sentence Stems* (page 38)
- *Write About It!* (page 39)

Additional Words

Introduce students to additional words such as *delectable*, *enticing*, *revolting*, *gross*, and *appealing* as you work through the lesson.

Answer Key

Vocabulary Ladders

Word	Definition
disgusting	looks and smells rotten; can make you sick
inedible	not able to be eaten; tastes bad
unappetizing	does not look or smell good enough to eat
bland	having little flavor or taste; plain
appetizing	looks and smells appealing
scrumptious	very pleasing to the senses; looks, smells, and tastes good
succulent	juicy and fresh; very tasty

Ordering Words

Check that students can explain why the words are ordered the way they are.

Sentence Clues

1. My morning oatmeal was (bland) because I forgot to add cinnamon to it.

2. The hot apple pie looked and smelled (succulent/scrumptious) sitting on the counter.

3. After I dropped my peanut butter and jelly sandwich on the floor it was (inedible/unappetizing).

4. My baby brother likes to eat dirt, which I find totally (disgusting).

5. Since I didn't get to eat lunch today, even meatloaf looked (appetizing) enough to eat.

Sentence Stems

Check that student responses reflect the meaning of the underlined word in each sentence frame.

Write About It!

Check that responses include the new vocabulary terms used in the correct way.

Name: _____ Date: _____

Activity Cards

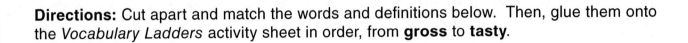

Directions: Cut apart and match the words and definitions below. Then, glue them onto the *Vocabulary Ladders* activity sheet in order, from **gross** to **tasty**.

appetizing	juicy and fresh; very tasty
bland	very pleasing to the senses; looks, smells, and tastes good
disgusting	looks and smells appealing
inedible	having little flavor or taste; plain
scrumptious	does not look or smell good enough to eat
succulent	not able to be eaten; tastes bad
unappetizing	looks and smells rotten; can make you sick

Name: _____ Date: _____

Ordering Words

Directions: Write the words from the Word Bank in the order you choose, from **gross** to **tasty**, on the ladder. Then, explain why you put them in the order you chose.

Word Bank

appetizing	bland	disgusting	inedible
scrumptious	succulent	unappetizing	

Explain why you ordered the words the way you did. You may use example sentences to help explain your thinking.

_____

_____

_____

_____

_____

_____

_____

_____

_____

_____

_____

Name: _____   Date: _____

Sentence Clues

Directions: Choose the best word from the Word Bank to complete each sentence.
Note: You may need to add or change the ending of a word to make it fit the sentence.

Word Bank

| appetizing | bland | disgusting | inedible |
| scrumptious | succulent | unappetizing | |

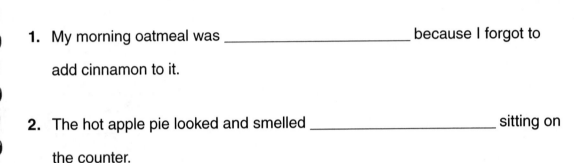

1. My morning oatmeal was _____ because I forgot to

    add cinnamon to it.

2. The hot apple pie looked and smelled _____ sitting on

    the counter.

3. After I dropped my peanut butter and jelly sandwich on the floor it was

    _____.

4. My baby brother likes to eat dirt, which I find totally _____.

5. Since I didn't get to eat lunch today, even meatloaf looked

    _____ enough to eat.

Directions: Create a fill-in-the-blank sentence on a separate sheet of
paper for at least one of the words in this lesson. Use the sentences
in the activity above as examples. Notice how a part of each sentence
provides a clue about which word fits best. Have a partner fill in the
missing word. Then, discuss why that word works best.

Name: _____ Date: _____

Sentence Stems

Directions: Complete each statement.

1. Three foods I think are <u>disgusting</u> are _____

   _____

   _____ .

2. The chocolate cake ended up being even more <u>scrumptious</u> when I added

   _____

   _____ .

3. Three foods I think are <u>bland</u> are _____

   _____

   _____ .

4. The hamburger became more <u>succulent</u> when I topped it with _____

   _____

   _____ .

5. Doctors say spinach may look <u>unappetizing</u> but it _____

   _____

   _____ .

#51305—*Vocabulary Ladders: Understanding Word Nuances*   © *Shell Education*

Name: _____   Date: _____

Write About It!

Directions: Read the prompt. Then, write a response. Underline the new vocabulary words you use in your response.

Write a compare and contrast essay about your favorite foods and your least favorite foods. Try to use as many of your new vocabulary words from the Word Bank as possible in your writing.

Word Bank

appetizing	bland	disgusting	
inedible	scrumptious	succulent	unappetizing

_____

_____

_____

_____

_____

_____

_____

_____

_____

_____

_____

_____

_____

Amount of Something

Teacher Note

For detailed instructions on how to implement the components of this lesson, see pages 15–19.

Objective

Students will analyze words related to the amount of something, from **a little** to **a lot**.

Materials

- *Vocabulary Ladders* template (page 142)
- *Activity Cards* (page 41)
- *Ordering Words* (page 42)
- *Sentence Clues* (page 43)
- *Sentence Stems* (page 44)
- *Write About It!* (page 45)

Additional Words

Introduce students to additional words such as *abundant*, *negligible*, *bountiful*, and *miniscule* as you work through the lesson.

Answer Key

Vocabulary Ladders

Word	Definition
scant	almost nonexistent
minute	extremely tiny
diminutive	very small; tiny
sufficient	enough; as much as needed
ample	more than enough to be satisfying
copious	very large quantity
exorbitant	an extremely large amount, well beyond what is reasonable

Ordering Words

Check that students can explain why the words are ordered the way they are.

Sentence Clues

1. The lawyer charged a(n) (exorbitant) fee for her services.

2. We had (ample/copius) food at the party because everyone brought a large dish to share.

3. We need to make sure there is a(n) (sufficient) amount of food for our backpacking trip.

4. The newborn baby held my finger with his (minute/diminutive) fingers.

5. After being stuck in the snowstorm for four more days than they expected, they were left with only a(n) (scant) amount of food.

Sentence Stems

Check that student responses reflect the meaning of the underlined word in each sentence frame.

Write About It!

Check that responses include the new vocabulary terms used in the correct way.

Name: _____   Date: _____

Activity Cards

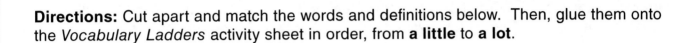

Directions: Cut apart and match the words and definitions below. Then, glue them onto the *Vocabulary Ladders* activity sheet in order, from **a little** to **a lot**.

ample	an extremely large amount, well beyond what is reasonable
copious	very large quantity
diminutive	more than enough to be satisfying
exorbitant	enough; as much as needed
minute	very small; tiny
scant	extremely tiny
sufficient	almost nonexistent

Name: _____   Date: _____

Ordering Words

Directions: Write the words from the Word Bank in the order you choose, from **a little** to **a lot**, on the ladder. Then, explain why you put them in the order you chose.

Word Bank

ample	copious	diminutive	exorbitant
minute	scant	sufficient	

Explain why you ordered the words the way you did. You may use example sentences to help explain your thinking.

_____

_____

_____

_____

_____

_____

_____

_____

_____

_____

Name: _____ Date: _____

Sentence Clues

Directions: Choose the best word from the Word Bank to complete each sentence.
Note: You may need to add or change the ending of a word to make it fit the sentence.

Word Bank

ample	copious	diminutive	exorbitant
minute	scant	sufficient	

1. The lawyer charged a(n) _____ fee for her services.

2. We had _____ food at the party because everyone brought a large dish to share.

3. We need to make sure there is a(n) _____ amount of food for our backpacking trip.

4. The newborn baby held my finger with his _____ fingers.

5. After being stuck in the snowstorm for four more days than they expected, they were left with only a(n) _____ amount of food.

Directions: Create a fill-in-the-blank sentence on a separate sheet of paper for at least one of the words in this lesson. Use the sentences in the activity above as examples. Notice how a part of each sentence provides a clue about which word fits best. Have a partner fill in the missing word. Then, discuss why that word works best.

Name: _____ Date: _____

Sentence Stems

Directions: Complete each statement.

1. I have <u>ample</u> time each day to _____

   _____

   _____ .

2. I decided my lunch was <u>sufficient</u> because I had _____

   _____

   _____ .

3. I feel <u>diminutive</u> when compared to _____

   _____

   _____ .

4. There are always <u>copious</u> amounts of food when I go to _____

   _____

   _____ .

5. Even a <u>minute</u> amount of money is worth donating to charity because

   _____

   _____ .

Name: _____ Date: _____

Write About It!

Directions: Read the prompt. Then, write a response. Underline the new vocabulary words you use in your response.

> Write a narrative about an encounter with someone who is less fortunate than you. Try to use as many of your new vocabulary words from the Word Bank as possible in your writing.

Word Bank			
ample	copious	diminutive	exorbitant
minute	scant	sufficient	

_____

_____

_____

_____

_____

_____

_____

_____

_____

_____

_____

_____

_____

Range of Emotion

Teacher Note

For detailed instructions on how to implement the components of this lesson, see pages 15–19.

Objective

Students will analyze words related to range of emotion, from **sad** to **happy**.

Materials

- *Vocabulary Ladders* template (page 142)
- *Activity Cards* (page 47)
- *Ordering Words* (page 48)
- *Sentence Clues* (page 49)
- *Sentence Stems* (page 50)
- *Write About It!* (page 51)

Additional Words

Introduce students to additional words such as *elated*, *morose*, *dismayed*, *content*, and *miserable* as you work through the lesson.

Answer Key

Vocabulary Ladders

Word	Definition
lugubrious	extreme sadness or mournful
downcast	unhappy or very sad
glum	in low spirits; sad or gloomy
satisfied	content; pleased with life
perky	lively and cheerful
giddy	very excited to the point of silliness
ecstatic	in a condition of extreme delight and overpowering happiness

Ordering Words

Check that students can explain why the words are ordered the way they are.

Sentence Clues

1. When the puppy ran away, the children were (downcast/glum).
2. He's been in a(n) (lugubrious) mood ever since his grandfather passed away.
3. Julie was (satisfied) with receiving mostly Bs on her report card.
4. The (perky) puppy ran to its master when he returned home from work.
5. Juan was (giddy/ecstatic) when he found the hundred-dollar bill on the ground.

Sentence Stems

Check that student responses reflect the meaning of the underlined word in each sentence frame.

Write About It!

Check that responses include the new vocabulary terms used in the correct way.

Name: _____   Date: _____

Activity Cards

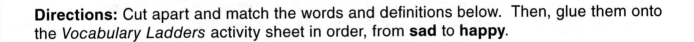

Directions: Cut apart and match the words and definitions below. Then, glue them onto the *Vocabulary Ladders* activity sheet in order, from **sad** to **happy**.

downcast	in a condition of extreme delight and overpowering happiness
ecstatic	very excited to the point of silliness
giddy	lively and cheerful
glum	content; pleased with life
lugubrious	in low spirits; sad or gloomy
perky	unhappy or very sad
satisfied	extreme sadness or mournful

Name: _____ Date: _____

Ordering Words

Directions: Write the words from the Word Bank in the order you choose, from **sad** to **happy**, on the ladder. Then, explain why you put them in the order you chose.

Word Bank

downcast	ecstatic	giddy	glum
lugubrious	perky	satisfied	

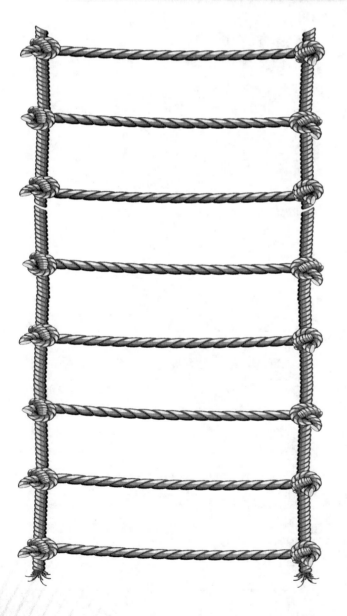

Explain why you ordered the words the way you did. You may use example sentences to help explain your thinking.

_____

_____

_____

_____

_____

_____

_____

_____

_____

_____

 #51305—*Vocabulary Ladders: Understanding Word Nuances*

Name: _____ Date: _____

Sentence Clues

Directions: Choose the best word from the Word Bank to complete each sentence.
Note: You may need to add or change the ending of a word to make it fit the sentence.

Word Bank

downcast	ecstatic	giddy	glum
lugubrious	perky	satisfied	

1. When the puppy ran away, the children were _____.

2. He's been in a(n) _____ mood ever since his grandfather passed away.

3. Julie was _____ with receiving mostly Bs on her report card.

4. The _____ puppy ran to its master when he returned home from work.

5. Juan was _____ when he found the hundred-dollar bill on the ground.

Directions: Create a fill-in-the-blank sentence on a separate sheet of paper for at least one of the words in this lesson. Use the sentences in the activity above as examples. Notice how a part of each sentence provides a clue about which word fits best. Have a partner fill in the missing word. Then, discuss why that word works best.

Name: _____   Date: _____

Sentence Stems

Directions: Complete each statement.

1. I might feel <u>lugubrious</u> if _____

   _____

   _____ .

2. Mom was in a <u>perky</u> mood, so she _____

   _____

   _____ .

3. I become <u>ecstatic</u> on the weekend when I get to _____

   _____

   _____ .

4. I sometimes feel <u>downcast</u> when _____

   _____

   _____ .

5. I am only <u>satisfied</u> with my homework when _____

   _____

   _____ .

Name: _____ Date: _____

Write About It!

Directions: Read the prompt. Then, write a response. Underline the new vocabulary words you use in your response.

Your class won a contest and the prize is a field trip anywhere the class wants to go. Your class has listed some suggestions on the board. You need to persuade your class/teacher to choose the destination of your choosing. Try to use as many of your new vocabulary words from the Word Bank as possible in your writing.

Word Bank

downcast	ecstatic	giddy	glum
lugubrious	perky	satisfied	

_____

_____

_____

_____

_____

_____

_____

_____

_____

_____

_____

_____

_____

_____

_____

To Ask

Teacher Note

For detailed instructions on how to implement the components of this lesson, see pages 15–19.

Objective

Students will analyze words related to asking, from **gently** to **forcefully**.

Materials

- *Vocabulary Ladders* template (page 142)
- *Activity Cards* (page 53)
- *Ordering Words* (page 54)
- *Sentence Clues* (page 55)
- *Sentence Stems* (page 56)
- *Write About It!* (page 57)

Additional Words

Introduce students to additional words such as *pester, snoop, interview, examine, harass,* and *research* as you work through the lesson.

Answer Key

Vocabulary Ladders

Word	Definition
inquire	to ask; to find out; to learn
quiz	to question in order to test knowledge
pry	to ask questions to uncover personal or secret information
nag	to bother by asking the same question repeatedly
probe	to question thoroughly
challenge	to ask questions in a persistent and doubtful manner
grill	to ask many questions in a harsh way for a long time

Ordering Words

Check that students can explain why the words are ordered the way they are.

Sentence Clues

1. My study partner wanted to (quiz/probe) me over the main ideas in the chapter before my big test.

2. My teacher thought it was a great idea to (grill/challenge) me in front of the whole class about the lesson since I wasn't paying attention.

3. Suzie wanted to know more about which girl Tony likes the best, so she decided to (pry) and ask him personal questions.

4. My little sister likes to (nag/grill) me all the time by continually asking me about my friends.

5. I decided to (inquire/probe) about the giraffes' day-to-day life at the zoo because I find them fascinating.

Sentence Stems

Check that student responses reflect the meaning of the underlined word in each sentence frame.

Write About It!

Check that responses include the new vocabulary terms used in the correct way.

Name: _____ Date: _____

Activity Cards

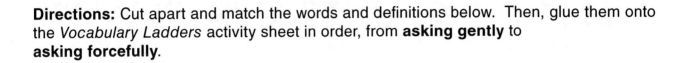

Directions: Cut apart and match the words and definitions below. Then, glue them onto the *Vocabulary Ladders* activity sheet in order, from **asking gently** to **asking forcefully**.

challenge	to ask many questions in a harsh way for a long time
grill	to ask questions in a persistent and doubtful manner
inquire	to question thoroughly
nag	to bother by asking the same question repeatedly
probe	to ask questions to uncover personal or secret information
pry	to question in order to test knowledge
quiz	to ask; to find out; to learn

Name: _____   Date: _____

Ordering Words

Directions: Write the words from the Word Bank in the order you choose, from **asking gently** to **forcefully**, on the ladder. Then, explain why you put them in the order you chose.

Word Bank			
challenge	grill	inquire	nag
probe	pry	quiz	

Explain why you ordered the words the way you did. You may use example sentences to help explain your thinking.

_____

_____

_____

_____

_____

_____

_____

_____

_____

_____

Name: _____ Date: _____

Sentence Clues

Directions: Choose the best word from the Word Bank to complete each sentence.
Note: You may need to add or change the ending of a word to make it fit the sentence.

Word Bank			
challenge	grill	inquire	nag
probe	pry	quiz	

1. My study partner wanted to _____ me over the main ideas in the chapter before my big test.

2. My teacher thought it was a great idea to _____ me in front of the whole class about the lesson since I wasn't paying attention.

3. Suzie wanted to know more about which girl Tony likes the best, so she decided to _____ and ask him personal questions.

4. My little sister likes to _____ me all the time by continually asking me about my friends.

5. I decided to _____ about the giraffes' day-to-day life at the zoo because I find them fascinating.

Directions: Create a fill-in-the-blank sentence on a separate sheet of paper for at least one of the words in this lesson. Use the sentences in the activity above as examples. Notice how a part of each sentence provides a clue about which word fits best. Have a partner fill in the missing word. Then, discuss why that word works best.

Name: _____ Date: _____

Sentence Stems

Directions: Complete each statement.

1. I am most often <u>nagged</u> about _____

_____

_____ .

2. Something I wouldn't be shy to <u>inquire</u> about is _____

_____

_____ .

3. The police officer <u>grilled</u> the suspect about _____

_____

_____ .

4. Kari and I <u>quizzed</u> each other about _____

_____

_____ .

5. I don't like when people <u>pry</u> because _____

_____

_____ .

Name: _____ Date: _____

Write About It!

Directions: Read the prompt. Then, write a response. Underline the new vocabulary words you use in your response.

Imagine you are a reporter and you have an opportunity to interview your favorite actor/actress. Describe the interview process. Try to use as many of your new vocabulary words from the Word Bank as possible in your writing.

Word Bank

challenge	grill	inquire	nag
probe	pry	quiz	

_____

_____

_____

_____

_____

_____

_____

_____

_____

_____

_____

Likeability

Teacher Note

For detailed instructions on how to implement the components of this lesson, see pages 15–19.

Objective

Students will analyze words related to likeability, from **dislike** to **enjoy**.

Materials

- *Vocabulary Ladders* template (page 142)

- *Activity Cards* (page 59)

- *Ordering Words* (page 60)

- *Sentence Clues* (page 61)

- *Sentence Stems* (page 62)

- *Write About It!* (page 63)

Additional Words

Introduce students to additional words such as *despise*, *admire*, and *enjoy* as you work through the lesson.

Answer Key

Vocabulary Ladders

Word	Definition
abhor	to have a complete and intense hatred for
loathe	to have a strong dislike for; hate
detest	to strongly dislike
favor	to have good feelings about; support
fancy	to like or be fond of
adore	to admire strongly
worship	to treat with much devotion or much love

Ordering Words

Check that students can explain why the words are ordered the way they are.

Sentence Clues

1. Many people (worship/adore) their teachers because they help them feel good about themselves when they are in class.

2. I (loathe/abhor) anyone who makes fun of or treats my family poorly.

3. Julie (favors) Ming for class president this year because he is a model student and a wonderful friend.

4. I (fancy) my brother's new girlfriend because she is kind to all our family.

5. Cassidy (detests) snakes because she is afraid of them.

Sentence Stems

Check that student responses reflect the meaning of the underlined word in each sentence frame.

Write About It!

Check that responses include the new vocabulary terms used in the correct way.

Name: _____ Date: _____

Activity Cards

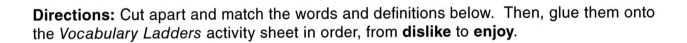

Directions: Cut apart and match the words and definitions below. Then, glue them onto the *Vocabulary Ladders* activity sheet in order, from **dislike** to **enjoy**.

abhor	to treat with much devotion or much love
adore	to admire strongly
detest	to like or be fond of
fancy	to have good feelings about; support
favor	to strongly dislike
loathe	to have a strong dislike for; hate
worship	to have a complete and intense hatred for

Name: _____ Date: _____

Ordering Words

Directions: Write the words from the Word Bank in the order you choose, from **dislike** to **enjoy**, on the ladder. Then, explain why you put them in the order you chose.

Word Bank

abhor	adore	detest	fancy
favor	loathe	worship	

Explain why you ordered the words the way you did. You may use example sentences to help explain your thinking.

_____

_____

_____

_____

_____

_____

_____

_____

_____

_____

_____

Name: _____ Date: _____

Sentence Clues

Directions: Choose the best word from the Word Bank to complete each sentence.
Note: You may need to add or change the ending of a word to make it fit the sentence.

Word Bank			
abhor	adore	detest	fancy
favor	loathe	worship	

1. Many people _____ their teachers because they help them feel good about themselves when they are in class.

2. I _____ anyone who makes fun of or treats my family poorly.

3. Julie _____ Ming for class president this year because he is a model student and a wonderful friend.

4. I _____ my brother's new girlfriend because she is kind to all our family.

5. Cassidy _____ snakes because she is afraid of them.

Directions: Create a fill-in-the-blank sentence on a separate sheet of paper for at least one of the words in this lesson. Use the sentences in the activity above as examples. Notice how a part of each sentence provides a clue about which word fits best. Have a partner fill in the missing word. Then, discuss why that word works best.

Name: _____   Date: _____

Sentence Stems

Directions: Complete each statement.

1. Three things I <u>loathe</u> eating are _____

_____

_____ .

2. I <u>favor</u> changes to my school such as _____

_____

_____ .

3. After school, I <u>detest</u> having to _____

_____

_____ .

4. I <u>adore</u> the way my best friend _____

_____

_____ .

5. I have taken a <u>fancy</u> to stores such as _____

_____

_____ .

Name: _____ Date: _____

Write About It!

Directions: Read the prompt. Then, write a response. Underline the new vocabulary words you use in your response.

Your school principal has decided to reduce the time for lunch by ten minutes in order to get more class time in. Write a letter to the principal indicating your thoughts about this idea. Try to use as many of your new vocabulary words from the Word Bank as possible in your writing.

Word Bank

abhor	adore	detest	fancy
favor	loathe	worship	

_____

_____

_____

_____

_____

_____

_____

_____

_____

_____

_____

_____

Said: Emotion

Teacher Note

For detailed instructions on how to implement the components of this lesson, see pages 15–19.

Objective

Students will analyze words related to emotion, from **upset** to **joyful**.

Materials

- *Vocabulary Ladders* template (page 142)
- *Activity Cards* (page 65)
- *Ordering Words* (page 66)
- *Sentence Clues* (page 67)
- *Sentence Stems* (page 68)
- *Write About It!* (page 69)

Additional Words

Introduce students to additional words such as *grieve, grunt, gloat,* and *grumble* as you work through the lesson.

Answer Key

Vocabulary Ladders

Word	Definition
seethe	to be very upset or angry
lament	to mourn for or regret
groan	to make a deep sound showing pain or sadness
bluster	to act in a loud way when upset
bumble	to speak in a clumsy way
whoop	to give a loud shout of laughter
exult	to rejoice greatly over some triumph

Ordering Words

Check that students can explain why the words are ordered the way they are.

Sentence Clues

1. John (seethed/blustered) about having to wait in line at the coffee shop.
2. It was hard for students to understand their teacher because he often (bumbled) through his lectures.
3. Cindy (exulted/whooped) when she received her perfect report card.
4. He sat in his room and (lamented) over the loss of his grandfather.
5. The class (groaned) loudly when their teacher handed out a pop quiz.

Sentence Stems

Check that student responses reflect the meaning of the underlined word in each sentence frame.

Write About It!

Check that responses include the new vocabulary terms used in the correct way.

Name: _____   Date: _____

Activity Cards

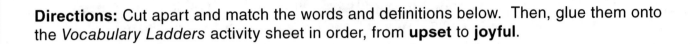

Directions: Cut apart and match the words and definitions below. Then, glue them onto the *Vocabulary Ladders* activity sheet in order, from **upset** to **joyful**.

bluster	to rejoice greatly over some triumph
bumble	to give a loud shout of laughter
exult	to speak in a clumsy way
groan	to act in a loud way when upset
lament	to make a deep sound showing pain or sadness
seethe	to mourn for or regret
whoop	to be very upset or angry

Name: _____   Date: _____

Ordering Words

Directions: Write the words from the Word Bank in the order you choose, from **upset** to **joyful**, on the ladder. Then, explain why you put them in the order you chose.

Word Bank			
bluster	bumble	exult	groan
lament	seethe	whoop	

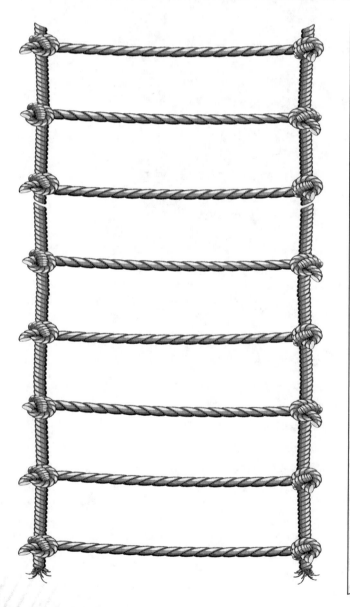

Explain why you ordered the words the way you did. You may use example sentences to help explain your thinking.

_____

_____

_____

_____

_____

_____

_____

_____

_____

_____

Name: _____ Date: _____

Sentence Clues

Directions: Choose the best word from the Word Bank to complete each sentence.
Note: You may need to add or change the ending of a word to make it fit the sentence.

Word Bank

bluster	bumble	exult	groan
lament	seethe	whoop	

1. John _____ about having to wait in line at the coffee shop.

2. It was hard for students to understand their teacher because he often _____ through his lectures.

3. Cindy _____ when she received her perfect report card.

4. He sat in his room and _____ over the loss of his grandfather.

5. The class _____ loudly when their teacher handed out a pop quiz.

Directions: Create a fill-in-the-blank sentence on a separate sheet of paper for at least one of the words in this lesson. Use the sentences in the activity above as examples. Notice how a part of each sentence provides a clue about which word fits best. Have a partner fill in the missing word. Then, discuss why that word works best.

Name: _____ Date: _____

Sentence Stems

Directions: Complete each statement.

1. I <u>seethe</u> when I am forced to _____

_____

_____ .

2. I would <u>lament</u> over the loss of _____

_____

_____ .

3. Two things that would cause me to <u>whoop</u> with joy are _____

_____

_____ .

4. I <u>groan</u> when I walk in the house if _____

_____

_____ .

5. The politician began to <u>bluster</u> about _____

_____

_____ .

Name: _____ Date: _____

Write About It!

Directions: Read the prompt. Then, write a response. Underline the new vocabulary words you use in your response.

Unfortunately, sometimes things do not go our way. Write about your idea of a not quite perfect day. Try to use as many of your new vocabulary words from the Word Bank as possible in your writing.

Word Bank

bluster	bumble	exult	groan
lament	seethe	whoop	

_____

_____

_____

_____

_____

_____

_____

_____

_____

_____

_____

_____

Move and Carry

Teacher Note

For detailed instructions on how to implement the components of this lesson, see pages 15–19.

Objective

Students will analyze words related to moving and carrying, from requiring **a little** to **a lot of effort**.

Materials

- *Vocabulary Ladders* template (page 142)
- *Activity Cards* (page 71)
- *Ordering Words* (page 72)
- *Sentence Clues* (page 73)
- *Sentence Stems* (page 74)
- *Write About It!* (page 75)

Additional Words

Introduce students to additional words such as *haul*, *yank*, *drag*, and *lift* as you work through the lesson.

Answer Key

Vocabulary Ladders

Word	Definition
tote	to carry on one's back or in arms or hands
schlep	to carry something slowly or awkwardly
lug	to pull or carry with effort
tow	to pull along at the end of a rope or chains
truck	to move heavy items back and forth with considerable effort
heft	to lift with a burst of effort
heave	to push up or out with great effort

Ordering Words

Check that students can explain why the words are ordered the way they are.

Sentence Clues

1. Lori (heaved/hefted) the heavy box onto the top shelf.

2. Diane carefully (schlepped) the dirty dishes to the kitchen because she didn't want to break them.

3. Larry (toted) his little brother on his back upstairs at bedtime.

4. I had to (lug/tow) Arnold, my St. Bernard, around the block because he refused to move after his nap.

5. All the rubbish was (trucked) out of our neighborhood this morning.

Sentence Stems

Check that student responses reflect the meaning of the underlined word in each sentence frame.

Write About It!

Check that responses include the new vocabulary terms used in the correct way.

Name: _____   Date: _____

Activity Cards

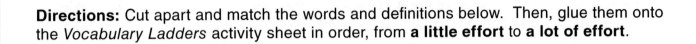

Directions: Cut apart and match the words and definitions below. Then, glue them onto the *Vocabulary Ladders* activity sheet in order, from **a little effort** to **a lot of effort**.

heave	to push up or out with great effort
heft	to lift with a burst of effort
lug	to move heavy items back and forth with considerable effort
schlep	to pull along at the end of a rope or chains
tote	to pull or carry with effort
tow	to carry something slowly or awkwardly
truck	to carry on one's back or in arms or hands

#51305—*Vocabulary Ladders: Understanding Word Nuances*   **71**

Name: _____ Date: _____

Ordering Words

Directions: Write the words from the Word Bank in the order you choose, from **a little effort** to **a lot of effort**, on the ladder. Then, explain why you put them in the order you chose.

Word Bank

heave	heft	lug	schlep
tote	tow	truck	

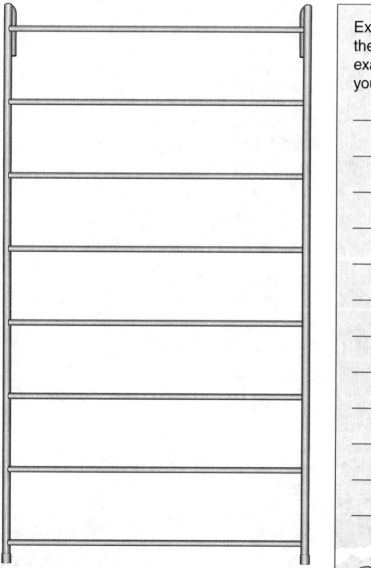

Explain why you ordered the words the way you did. You may use example sentences to help explain your thinking.

_____

_____

_____

_____

_____

_____

_____

_____

_____

_____

_____

#51305—*Vocabulary Ladders: Understanding Word Nuances* © *Shell Education*

Name: _____   Date: _____

Sentence Clues

Directions: Choose the best word from the Word Bank to complete each sentence.
Note: You may need to add or change the ending of a word to make it fit the sentence.

Word Bank

heave	heft	lug	schlep
tote	tow	truck	

---

1. Lori _____ the heavy box onto the top shelf.

2. Diane carefully _____ the dirty dishes to the kitchen because she didn't want to break them.

3. Larry _____ his little brother on his back upstairs at bedtime.

4. I had to _____ Arnold, my St. Bernard, around the block because he refused to move after his nap.

5. All the rubbish was _____ out of our neighborhood this morning.

Directions: Create a fill-in-the-blank sentence on a separate sheet of paper for at least one of the words in this lesson. Use the sentences in the activity above as examples. Notice how a part of each sentence provides a clue about which word fits best. Have a partner fill in the missing word. Then, discuss why that word works best.

Name: _____ Date: _____

Sentence Stems

Directions: Complete each statement.

1. When we picked up my brother at the airport, I had to <u>schlep</u>

   _____

   _____ .

2. My backpack is heavy to <u>tote</u> when it is filled with _____

   _____

   _____ .

3. The burly sailors were able to <u>heave</u> _____

   _____

   _____ .

4. The weight lifter was able to <u>heft</u> _____

   _____

   _____ .

5. When we move to a new town, we will <u>truck</u> _____

   _____

   _____ .

Name: _____ Date: _____

Write About It!

Directions: Read the prompt. Then, write a response. Underline the new vocabulary words you use in your response.

Your family has moved to a new home. Describe moving day for your family and whether or not your family members worked together or if there was any trouble. Try to use as many of your new vocabulary words from the Word Bank as possible in your writing.

Word Bank

heave	heft	lug	schlep
tote	tow	truck	

_____

_____

_____

_____

_____

_____

_____

_____

_____

_____

_____

_____

Direction of Travel

Teacher Note

For detailed instructions on how to implement the components of this lesson, see pages 15–19.

Objective

Students will analyze words related to direction of travel, from **up** to **down**.

Materials

- *Vocabulary Ladders* template (page 142)

- *Activity Cards* (page 77)

- *Ordering Words* (page 78)

- *Sentence Clues* (page 79)

- *Sentence Stems* (page 80)

- *Write About It!* (page 81)

Additional Words

Introduce students to additional words such as *descend, plunge, escalate, boost,* and *rise* as you work through the lesson.

Answer Key

Vocabulary Ladders

Word	Definition
skyrocket	to rise up at extreme speeds
soar	to fly or glide at a great height
ascend	to climb or go upward
raise	to move to a higher position
decline	to slope or slant downward
sink	to fall or drop slowly
plummet	to fall sharply down at a high speed

Ordering Words

Check that students can explain why the words are ordered the way they are.

Sentence Clues

1. The submarine must (ascend) at a slow pace as it rises to the surface.

2. My little brother likes to push down and (sink) his boats in the bathtub.

3. You need to (raise) your glass of sparkling cider during the toast.

4. Paul watched his toy rocket ship (soar/skyrocket) into the air after his dad launched it.

5. When Steve decided to play hours and hours of video games, his grades began to (plummet/decline).

Sentence Stems

Check that student responses reflect the meaning of the underlined word in each sentence frame.

Write About It!

Check that responses include the new vocabulary terms used in the correct way.

Name: _____ Date: _____

Activity Cards

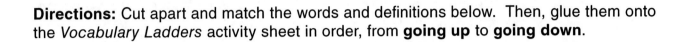

Directions: Cut apart and match the words and definitions below. Then, glue them onto the *Vocabulary Ladders* activity sheet in order, from **going up** to **going down**.

ascend	to rise up at extreme speeds
decline	to fly or glide at a great height
plummet	to climb or go upward
raise	to move to a higher position
sink	to slope or slant downward
skyrocket	to fall or drop slowly
soar	to fall sharply down at a high speed

Name: _____ Date: _____

Ordering Words

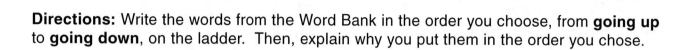

Directions: Write the words from the Word Bank in the order you choose, from **going up** to **going down**, on the ladder. Then, explain why you put them in the order you chose.

Word Bank			
ascend	decline	plummet	raise
sink	skyrocket	soar	

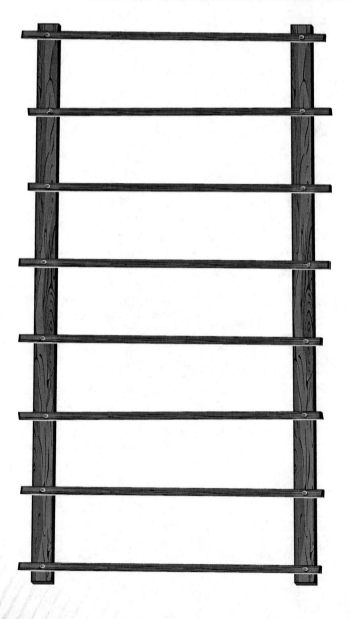

Explain why you ordered the words the way you did. You may use example sentences to help explain your thinking.

_____

_____

_____

_____

_____

_____

_____

_____

_____

_____

Name: _____   Date: _____

Sentence Clues

Directions: Choose the best word from the Word Bank to complete each sentence.
Note: You may need to add or change the ending of a word to make it fit the sentence.

Word Bank

ascend	decline	plummet	raise
sink	skyrocket	soar	

---

1. The submarine must _____ at a slow pace as it rises

   to the surface.

2. My little brother likes to push down and _____ his

   boats in the bathtub.

3. You need to _____ your glass of sparkling cider during

   the toast.

4. Paul watched his toy rocket ship _____ into the air

   after his dad launched it.

5. When Steve decided to play hours and hours of video games, his grades

   began to _____.

Directions: Create a fill-in-the-blank sentence on a separate sheet of paper for at least one of the words in this lesson. Use the sentences in the activity above as examples. Notice how a part of each sentence provides a clue about which word fits best. Have a partner fill in the missing word. Then, discuss why that word works best.

Name: _____ Date: _____

Sentence Stems

Directions: Complete each statement.

1. My attitude <u>plummets</u> when _____

   _____

   _____ .

2. As the plane <u>soared</u> over the stadium _____

   _____

   _____ .

3. Three things that would likely <u>sink</u> in a tub of water are _____

   _____

   _____ .

4. In order to <u>raise</u> my grades, I would need to _____

   _____

   _____ .

5. My grades would start to <u>decline</u> if _____

   _____

   _____ .

Name: _____   Date: _____

Write About It!

Directions: Read the prompt. Then, write a response. Underline the new vocabulary words you use in your response.

Describe a day at your favorite amusement park. How was the weather? How were the rides? Try to use as many of your new vocabulary words from the Word Bank as possible in your writing.

Word Bank

ascend	decline	plummet	raise
sink	skyrocket	soar	

_____

_____

_____

_____

_____

_____

_____

_____

_____

_____

_____

_____

_____

Moving Forward

Teacher Note

For detailed instructions on how to implement the components of this lesson, see pages 15–19.

Objective

Students will analyze words related to moving forward, from **slowly** to **quickly**.

Materials

- *Vocabulary Ladders* template (page 142)

- *Activity Cards* (page 83)

- *Ordering Words* (page 84)

- *Sentence Clues* (page 85)

- *Sentence Stems* (page 86)

- *Write About It!* (page 87)

Additional Words

Introduce students to additional words such as *dawdle, hurtle, gallop,* and *bolt* as you work through the lesson.

Answer Key

Vocabulary Ladders

Word	Definition
lag	to fall behind; to move at an extremely slow pace
mosey	to walk slowly or aimlessly
traipse	to walk or wander at a casual pace
saunter	to walk at an unhurried pace
jog	to run at an easy, comfortable pace
charge	to rush ahead at an object
stampede	sudden, fast movement out of fear, often with others

Ordering Words

Check that students can explain why the words are ordered the way they are.

Sentence Clues

1. Rachel and Maya slowly (sauntered/moseyed) into class after recess.

2. The excited students (stampeded/charged) out the door on the last day of school.

3. George (lagged) behind after lunch because he was not excited about the upcoming test.

4. I like to (jog) with my dad because he runs at an easy pace to keep up with.

5. My dog (traipsed/sauntered) around the park during our daily walk.

Sentence Stems

Check that student responses reflect the meaning of the underlined word in each sentence frame.

Write About It!

Check that responses include the new vocabulary terms used in the correct way.

Name: _____ Date: _____

Activity Cards

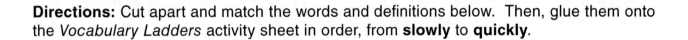

Directions: Cut apart and match the words and definitions below. Then, glue them onto the *Vocabulary Ladders* activity sheet in order, from **slowly** to **quickly**.

charge	sudden, fast movement out of fear, often with others
jog	to rush ahead at an object
lag	to run at an easy, comfortable pace
mosey	to walk at an unhurried pace
saunter	to walk or wander at a casual pace
stampede	to walk slowly or aimlessly
traipse	to fall behind; to move at an extremely slow pace

#51305—*Vocabulary Ladders: Understanding Word Nuances*

Name: _____   Date: _____

Ordering Words

Directions: Write the words from the Word Bank in the order you choose, from **slow** to **quick**, on the ladder. Then, explain why you put them in the order you chose.

Word Bank

charge	jog	lag	mosey
saunter	stampede	traipse	

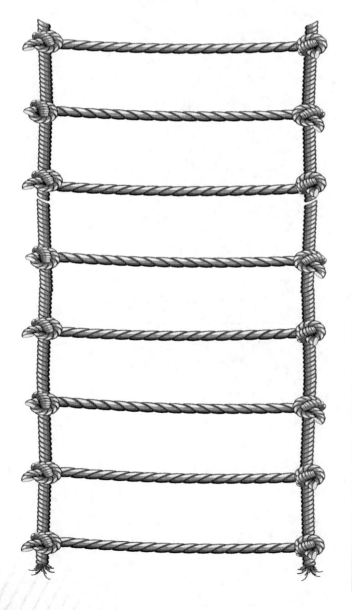

Explain why you ordered the words the way you did. You may use example sentences to help explain your thinking.

_____

_____

_____

_____

_____

_____

_____

_____

_____

_____

Name: _____   Date: _____

Sentence Clues

Directions: Choose the best word from the Word Bank to complete each sentence.
Note: You may need to add or change the ending of a word to make it fit the sentence.

Word Bank

charge	jog	lag	mosey
saunter	stampede	traipse	

1. Rachel and Maya slowly _____ into class after recess.

2. The excited students _____ out the door on the last day of school.

3. George _____ behind after lunch because he was not excited about the upcoming test.

4. I like to _____ with my dad because he runs at at easy pace to keep up with.

5. My dog _____ around the park during our daily walk.

Directions: Create a fill-in-the-blank sentence on a separate sheet of paper for at least one of the words in this lesson. Use the sentences in the activity above as examples. Notice how a part of each sentence provides a clue about which word fits best. Have a partner fill in the missing word. Then, discuss why that word works best.

Name: _____ Date: _____

Sentence Stems

Directions: Complete each statement.

1. The woman was happy as she <u>moseyed</u> through the flower garden because

_____

_____ .

2. Elephants would <u>stampede</u> through the jungle if _____

_____

_____ .

3. I might <u>charge</u> through the front door if _____

_____

_____ .

4. The students in my class would <u>saunter</u> around the field if _____

_____

_____ .

5. I like to <u>lag</u> behind everyone else only when _____

_____

_____ .

Name: _____   Date: _____

Write About It!

Directions: Read the prompt. Then, write a response. Underline the new vocabulary words you use in your response.

Everyone likes to do different things when they go to the park. Explain what you like to do when you go. Try to use as many of your new vocabulary words from the Word Bank as possible in your writing.

Word Bank			
charge	jog	lag	
mosey	saunter	stampede	traipse

#51305—Vocabulary Ladders: Understanding Word Nuances

Personal Attitude or Appearance

Teacher Note

For detailed instructions on how to implement the components of this lesson, see pages 15–19.

Objective

Students will analyze words related to personal attitude or appearance, from **weak** to **strong**.

Materials

- *Vocabulary Ladders* template (page 142)
- *Activity Cards* (page 89)
- *Ordering Words* (page 90)
- *Sentence Clues* (page 91)
- *Sentence Stems* (page 92)
- *Write About It!* (page 93)

Additional Words

Introduce students to additional words such as *apathetic, dynamic, influential, listless, powerful,* and *puny* as you work through the lesson.

Answer Key

Vocabulary Ladders

Word	Definition
slothful	very lazy and slow
sluggish	lazy or without energy
feeble	without strength; weak in body or mind
firm	strong and solid
intense	very strong
forceful	having great power or effectiveness
vigorous	extremely strong, forceful, and enthusiastic

Ordering Words

Check that students can explain why the words are ordered the way they are.

Sentence Clues

1. Todd's (sluggish/slothful) response let Jackie know that he was tired.

2. The debate over the correct answer between the students was (intense/vigorous).

3. Mom's response of "no" was pretty (firm) when I asked her if I could stay at Tracy's house for another hour.

4. The lawyer's (forceful/vigorous) argument for the defendant impressed the jury.

5. Jack's answer sounded (feeble) because he knew it was incorrect.

Sentence Stems

Check that student responses reflect the meaning of the underlined word in each sentence frame.

Write About It!

Check that responses include the new vocabulary terms used in the correct way.

Name: _____ Date: _____

Activity Cards

Directions: Cut apart and match the words and definitions below. Then, glue them onto the *Vocabulary Ladders* activity sheet in order, from **weak** to **strong**.

feeble	extremely strong, forceful, and enthusiastic
firm	having great power or effectiveness
forceful	very strong
intense	strong and solid
slothful	without strength; weak in body or mind
sluggish	lazy or without energy
vigorous	very lazy and slow

Name: _____   Date: _____

Ordering Words

Directions: Write the words from the Word Bank in the order you choose, from **weak** to **strong**, on the ladder. Then, explain why you put them in the order you chose.

Word Bank

feeble	firm	forceful	intense
slothful	sluggish	vigorous	

Explain why you ordered the words the way you did. You may use example sentences to help explain your thinking.

_____

_____

_____

_____

_____

_____

_____

_____

_____

_____

Name: _____ Date: _____

Sentence Clues

Directions: Choose the best word from the Word Bank to complete each sentence.
Note: You may need to add or change the ending of a word to make it fit the sentence.

Word Bank			
feeble	firm	forceful	intense
slothful	sluggish	vigorous	

1. Todd's _____ response let Jackie know that he was tired.

2. The debate over the correct answer between the students was

   _____.

3. Mom's response of "no" was pretty _____ when I asked

   her if I could stay at Tracy's house for another hour.

4. The lawyer's _____ argument for the defendant impressed

   the jury.

5. Jack's answer sounded _____ because he knew it was

   incorrect.

Directions: Create a fill-in-the-blank sentence on a separate sheet of
paper for at least one of the words in this lesson. Use the sentences
in the activity above as examples. Notice how a part of each sentence
provides a clue about which word fits best. Have a partner fill in the
missing word. Then, discuss why that word works best.

Name: _____   Date: _____

Sentence Stems

Directions: Complete each statement.

1. My dog shook <u>vigorously</u> after _____

   _____

   _____ .

2. The police officer was <u>forceful</u> when he talked with the students about

   _____

   _____ .

3. After an <u>intense</u> conversation with my best friend, I might feel _____

   _____

   _____ .

4. I respond in a <u>feeble</u> way if I am feeling _____

   _____

   _____ .

5. My teacher uses a <u>firm</u> voice when _____

   _____

   _____ .

Name: _____ Date: _____

Write About It!

Directions: Read the prompt. Then, write a response. Underline the new vocabulary words you use in your response.

Imagine you were chosen to debate whether or not students in your school should wear school uniforms. Describe how you and your opponent tackled this controversial issue. Try to use as many of your new vocabulary words from the Word Bank as possible in your writing.

Word Bank

| feeble | firm | forceful | |
| intense | slothful | sluggish | vigorous |

_____

_____

_____

_____

_____

_____

_____

_____

_____

_____

_____

Level of Difficulty in Work

Teacher Note

For detailed instructions on how to implement the components of this lesson, see pages 15–19.

Objective

Students will analyze words related to level of difficulty in work, from **easy** to **hard**.

Materials

- *Vocabulary Ladders* template (page 142)
- *Activity Cards* (page 95)
- *Ordering Words* (page 96)
- *Sentence Clues* (page 97)
- *Sentence Stems* (page 98)
- *Write About It!* (page 99)

Additional Words

Introduce students to additional words such as *taxing, laborious, simple,* and *harsh* as you work through the lesson.

Answer Key

Vocabulary Ladders

Word	Definition
effortless	requiring little to no effort
facile	acting or working in an easy and productive manner
undemanding	does not require much attention and effort
manageable	capable of being handled
demanding	requiring urgent attention and effort
grueling	very tiring or difficult
arduous	involving great difficulty or endurance

Ordering Words

Check that students can explain why the words are ordered the way they are.

Sentence Clues

1. If it weren't for the (arduous/grueling) work of the firefighters, my neighbors would have lost their home.

2. Madu thought this week's homework load was (manageable) because it didn't take him very long to complete.

3. The ballerina made her routine look (facile/effortless) as she moved with such grace and poise.

4. Mike's (undemanding) schedule allowed him to meet up with friends he hadn't seen in a while.

5. Alicia only had a five-minute lunch break due to her (demanding) boss.

Sentence Stems

Check that student responses reflect the meaning of the underlined word in each sentence frame.

Write About It!

Check that responses include the new vocabulary terms used in the correct way.

Name: _____   Date: _____

Activity Cards

Directions: Cut apart and match the words and definitions below. Then, glue them onto the *Vocabulary Ladders* activity sheet in order, from **easy** to **hard**.

arduous	involving great difficulty or endurance
demanding	very tiring or difficult
effortless	requiring urgent attention and effort
facile	capable of being handled
grueling	does not require much attention and effort
manageable	acting or working in an easy and productive manner
undemanding	requiring little to no effort

Name: _____ Date: _____

Ordering Words

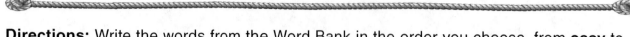

Directions: Write the words from the Word Bank in the order you choose, from **easy** to **hard**, on the ladder. Then, explain why you put them in the order you chose.

Word Bank

arduous	demanding	effortless	facile
grueling	manageable	undemanding	

Explain why you ordered the words the way you did. You may use example sentences to help explain your thinking.

_____

_____

_____

_____

_____

_____

_____

_____

_____

_____

Name: _____ Date: _____

Sentence Clues

Directions: Choose the best word from the Word Bank to complete each sentence.
Note: You may need to add or change the ending of a word to make it fit the sentence.

Word Bank			
arduous	demanding	effortless	facile
grueling	manageable	undemanding	

1. If it weren't for the _____ work of the firefighters, my neighbors would have lost their home.

2. Madu thought this week's homework load was _____ because it didn't take him very long to complete.

3. The ballerina made her routine look _____ as she moved with such grace and poise.

4. Mike's _____ schedule allowed him to meet up with friends he hadn't seen in a while.

5. Alicia only had a five-minute lunch break due to her _____ boss.

Directions: Create a fill-in-the-blank sentence on a separate sheet of paper for at least one of the words in this lesson. Use the sentences in the activity above as examples. Notice how a part of each sentence provides a clue about which word fits best. Have a partner fill in the missing word. Then, discuss why that word works best.

Name: _____ Date: _____

Sentence Stems

Directions: Complete each statement.

1. My teacher can be <u>demanding</u> when _____

   _____

   _____ .

2. A test might be a <u>grueling</u> experience for me if _____

   _____

   _____ .

3. Although I have a busy schedule, it is <u>manageable</u> because _____

   _____

   _____ .

4. Three <u>arduous</u> chores for me are _____

   _____

   _____ .

5. When my teacher is <u>undemanding</u>, it makes it easy to _____

   _____

   _____ .

Name: _____ Date: _____

Write About It!

Directions: Read the prompt. Then, write a response. Underline the new vocabulary words you use in your response.

Think about a time when you learned a new skill. Describe the skill and how easy or difficult it was to learn. Try to use as many of your new vocabulary words from the Word Bank as possible in your writing.

Word Bank

arduous	demanding	effortless	
facile	grueling	manageable	undemanding

_____
_____
_____
_____
_____
_____
_____
_____
_____
_____
_____
_____

Level of Interest

Teacher Note

For detailed instructions on how to implement the components of this lesson, see pages 15–19.

Objective

Students will analyze words related to level of interest, from **boring** to **interesting**.

Materials

- *Vocabulary Ladders* template (page 142)

- *Activity Cards* (page 101)

- *Ordering Words* (page 102)

- *Sentence Clues* (page 103)

- *Sentence Stems* (page 104)

- *Write About It!* (page 105)

Additional Words

Introduce students to additional words such as *tedious, entrancing, gripping, fascinate,* and *incredible* as you work through the lesson.

Answer Key

Vocabulary Ladders

Word	Definition
mindless	requires little intelligence or effort
monotonous	not interesting because of having to do the same thing over and over
ho-hum	indifference and boredom; no interest
routine	regular everyday activities
stimulating	able to arouse attention and interest
compelling	strong hold on a person's attention
captivating	charming and fascinating; very interesting

Ordering Words

Check that students can explain why the words are ordered the way they are.

Sentence Clues

1. Her data entry job seems (mindless) because there is not a lot of thought required.

2. The (compelling/captivating) acrobatic performance kept all the students' attention.

3. The (stimulating) lesson on Newton's First Law generated numerous questions and discussions.

4. The professor's (ho-hum/monotonous) voice put a few students to sleep.

5. Angela's (routine) visits to the nursing home brought daily smiles.

Sentence Stems

Check that student responses reflect the meaning of the underlined word in each sentence frame.

Write About It!

Check that responses include the new vocabulary terms used in the correct way.

Name: _____ Date: _____

Activity Cards

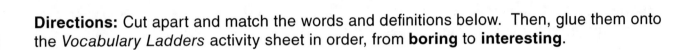

Directions: Cut apart and match the words and definitions below. Then, glue them onto the *Vocabulary Ladders* activity sheet in order, from **boring** to **interesting**.

captivating	charming and fascinating; very interesting
compelling	strong hold on a person's attention
ho-hum	able to arouse attention and interest
mindless	regular everyday activities
monotonous	indifference and boredom; no interest
routine	not interesting because of having to do the same thing over and over
stimulating	requires little intelligence or effort

Name: _____ Date: _____

Ordering Words

Directions: Write the words from the Word Bank in the order you choose, from **boring** to **interesting**, on the ladder. Then, explain why you put them in the order you chose.

> **Word Bank**
>
> captivating   compelling   ho-hum   mindless
> monotonous   routine   stimulating

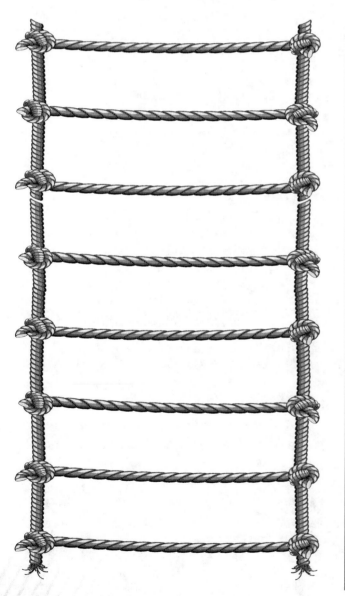

Explain why you ordered the words the way you did. You may use example sentences to help explain your thinking.

_____

_____

_____

_____

_____

_____

_____

_____

_____

_____

Name: _____ Date: _____

Sentence Clues

Directions: Choose the best word from the Word Bank to complete each sentence.
Note: You may need to add or change the ending of a word to make it fit the sentence.

Word Bank

captivating	compelling	ho-hum	mindless
monotonous	routine	stimulating	

---

1. Her data entry job seems _____ because there is not a lot of thought required.

2. The _____ acrobatic performance kept all the students' attention.

3. The _____ lesson on Newton's First Law generated numerous questions and discussions.

4. The professor's _____ voice put a few students to sleep.

5. Angela's _____ visits to the nursing home brought daily smiles.

Directions: Create a fill-in-the-blank sentence on a separate sheet of paper for at least one of the words in this lesson. Use the sentences in the activity above as examples. Notice how a part of each sentence provides a clue about which word fits best. Have a partner fill in the missing word. Then, discuss why that word works best.

Name: _____   Date: _____

Sentence Stems

Directions: Complete each statement.

1. The <u>routine</u> chores I do on a constant basis are _____

    _____

    _____ .

2. Tom says that his job is <u>mindless</u> because _____

    _____

    _____ .

3. Something on television that would <u>captivate</u> me would be _____

    _____

    _____ .

4. Sometimes my life might seem <u>monotonous</u> because _____

    _____

    _____ .

5. I would find a concert <u>compelling</u> if _____

    _____

    _____ .

Name: _____ Date: _____

Write About It!

Directions: Read the prompt. Then, write a response. Underline the new vocabulary words you use in your response.

Imagine that you have an opportunity to be a teacher for a day. Write about how your day would go. Try to use as many of your new vocabulary words from the Word Bank as possible in your writing.

Word Bank

captivating	compelling	ho-hum	mindless
monotonous	routine	stimulating	

_____

_____

_____

_____

_____

_____

_____

_____

_____

_____

_____

_____

_____

_____

Entertainment

Teacher Note

For detailed instructions on how to implement the components of this lesson, see pages 15–19.

Objective

Students will analyze words related to entertainment, from **serious** to **funny**.

Materials

- *Vocabulary Ladders* template (page 142)

- *Activity Cards* (page 107)

- *Ordering Words* (page 108)

- *Sentence Clues* (page 109)

- *Sentence Stems* (page 110)

- *Write About It!* (page 111)

Additional Words

Introduce students to additional words such as *dreadful, somber, uproarious,* and *whimsical* as you work through the lesson.

Answer Key

Vocabulary Ladders

Word	Definition
tragic	deep sadness or distress
melancholy	a feeling of sadness or depression
solemn	a serious or grave mood
amusing	to cause time to pass pleasantly
humorous	pleasantly funny
comical	very funny; elicits laughter
hilarious	extremely funny and amusing; rolling laughter

Ordering Words

Check that students can explain why the words are ordered the way they are.

Sentence Clues

1. Gary's Halloween costume was (amusing/comical), which brought lots of smiles and giggles.

2. Leonard was in a(n) (solemn/melancholy) mood when he brought his poor report card home.

3. The (tragic/melancholy) mood was felt by everyone at the funeral.

4. The comedian at the school talent show was (humorous/amusing/hilarious).

5. The class burst out with laughter at Kate's (hilarious) joke.

Sentence Stems

Check that student responses reflect the meaning of the underlined word in each sentence frame.

Write About It!

Check that responses include the new vocabulary terms used in the correct way.

Name: _____ Date: _____

Activity Cards

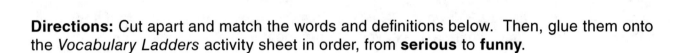

Directions: Cut apart and match the words and definitions below. Then, glue them onto the *Vocabulary Ladders* activity sheet in order, from **serious** to **funny**.

amusing	extremely funny and amusing; rolling laughter
comical	very funny; elicits laughter
hilarious	pleasantly funny
humorous	to cause time to pass pleasantly
melancholy	a serious or grave mood
solemn	a feeling of sadness or depression
tragic	deep sadness or distress

Name: _____   Date: _____

Ordering Words

Directions: Write the words from the Word Bank in the order you choose, from **serious** to **funny**, on the ladder. Then, explain why you put them in the order you chose.

Word Bank

amusing	comical	hilarious	humorous
melancholy	solemn	tragic	

Explain why you ordered the words the way you did. You may use example sentences to help explain your thinking.

_____

_____

_____

_____

_____

_____

_____

_____

_____

_____

_____

Name: _____   Date: _____

Sentence Clues

Directions: Choose the best word from the Word Bank to complete each sentence.
Note: You may need to add or change the ending of a word to make it fit the sentence.

Word Bank

amusing	comical	hilarious	humorous
melancholy	solemn	tragic	

1. Gary's Halloween costume was _____, which brought lots of smiles and giggles.

2. Leonard was in a(n) _____ mood when he brought his poor report card home.

3. The _____ mood was felt by everyone at the funeral.

4. The comedian at the school talent show was _____.

5. The class burst out with laughter at Kate's _____ joke.

Directions: Create a fill-in-the-blank sentence on a separate sheet of paper for at least one of the words in this lesson. Use the sentences in the activity above as examples. Notice how a part of each sentence provides a clue about which word fits best. Have a partner fill in the missing word. Then, discuss why that word works best.

Name: _____ Date: _____

Sentence Stems

Directions: Complete each statement.

1. I find myself in a <u>solemn</u> mood when _____

_____

_____ .

2. If someone tells me a <u>comical</u> story, it makes me feel _____

_____

_____ .

3. In order for a television show to be <u>humorous</u> to me, it must _____

_____

_____ .

4. The team was clearly in a <u>melancholy</u> mood; it had just _____

_____

_____ .

5. Other people find me <u>amusing</u> when _____

_____

_____ .

Name: _____ Date: _____

Write About It!

Directions: Read the prompt. Then, write a response. Underline the new vocabulary words you use in your response.

Imagine that you spent an entire day with your favorite person. Write about how your day would go. Try to use as many of your new vocabulary words from the Word Bank as possible in your writing.

Word Bank

amusing	comical	hilarious	
humorous	melancholy	solemn	tragic

Showing Interest

Teacher Note

For detailed instructions on how to implement the components of this lesson, see pages 15–19.

Objective

Students will analyze words related to showing interest, from **disinterested** to **interested**.

Materials

- *Vocabulary Ladders* template (page 142)
- *Activity Cards* (page 113)
- *Ordering Words* (page 114)
- *Sentence Clues* (page 115)
- *Sentence Stems* (page 116)
- *Write About It!* (page 117)

Additional Words

Introduce students to additional words such as *avid, fervent, lethargic, ambitious*, and *committed* as you work through the lesson.

Answer Key

Vocabulary Ladders

Word	Definition
disenchanted	having totally lost interest; discouraged; disconnected
apathetic	having or displaying little concern or interest
passive	not responding to something that might affect a person
concerned	affected or troubled by a situation
engaged	showing sustained interest in a particular activity
passionate	having or showing strong emotions
zealous	filled with intense enthusiasm toward a cause or purpose

Ordering Words

Check that students can explain why the words are ordered the way they are.

Sentence Clues

1. The (apathetic) police officer showed no sympathy when the woman started crying over her speeding ticket.

2. The students were (engaged/concerned) as they listened carefully to the speaker at the assembly this afternoon.

3. The candidate's (zealous/passionate) supporters worked all night long stuffing envelopes.

4. May was (disenchanted) about dating after hearing of her best friend's broken heart.

5. Displaying no emotion, she remained (passive) when the bully called her names.

Sentence Stems

Check that student responses reflect the meaning of the underlined word in each sentence frame.

Write About It!

Check that responses include the new vocabulary terms used in the correct way.

Name: _____   Date: _____

Activity Cards

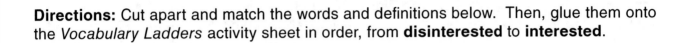

Directions: Cut apart and match the words and definitions below. Then, glue them onto the *Vocabulary Ladders* activity sheet in order, from **disinterested** to **interested**.

apathetic	filled with intense enthusiasm toward a cause or purpose
concerned	having or showing strong emotions
disenchanted	showing sustained interest in a particular activity
engaged	affected or troubled by a situation
passionate	not responding to something that might affect a person
passive	having or displaying little concern or interest
zealous	having totally lost interest; discouraged; disconnected

Name: _____   Date: _____

Ordering Words

Directions: Write the words from the Word Bank in the order you choose, from **disinterested** to **interested**, on the ladder. Then, explain why you put them in the order you chose.

Word Bank

apathetic	concerned	disenchanted	engaged
passionate	passive	zealous	

Explain why you ordered the words the way you did. You may use example sentences to help explain your thinking.

_____

_____

_____

_____

_____

_____

_____

_____

_____

Name: _____ Date: _____

Sentence Clues

Directions: Choose the best word from the Word Bank to complete each sentence.
Note: You may need to add or change the ending of a word to make it fit the sentence.

Word Bank

apathetic	concerned	disenchanted	engaged
passionate	passive	zealous	

---

1. The _____ police officer showed no sympathy when the woman started crying over her speeding ticket.

2. The students were _____ as they listened carefully to the speaker at the assembly this afternoon.

3. The candidate's _____ supporters worked all night long stuffing envelopes.

4. May was _____ about dating after hearing of her best friend's broken heart.

5. Displaying no emotion, she remained _____ when the bully called her names.

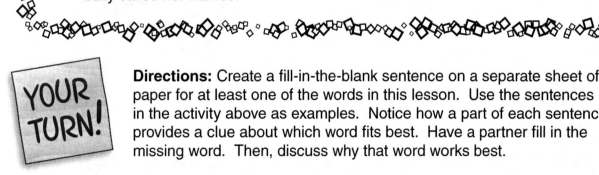

Directions: Create a fill-in-the-blank sentence on a separate sheet of paper for at least one of the words in this lesson. Use the sentences in the activity above as examples. Notice how a part of each sentence provides a clue about which word fits best. Have a partner fill in the missing word. Then, discuss why that word works best.

Name: _____   Date: _____

Sentence Stems

Directions: Complete each statement.

1. Three things I am <u>passionate</u> about in life are _____

   _____

   _____ .

2. Although I like to act in school plays, I might feel <u>disenchanted</u> if

   _____

   _____ .

3. Our teacher says that we should not be <u>apathetic</u> about _____

   _____

   _____ .

4. The students in my class are always <u>engaged</u> when _____

   _____

   _____ .

5. Three things parents are often <u>concerned</u> about are _____

   _____

   _____ .

Name: _____ Date: _____

Write About It!

Directions: Read the prompt. Then, write a response. Underline the new vocabulary words you use in your response.

> Your school invited a magician to perform at your school assembly. Write about your experience as a participant in the show. Try to use as many of your new vocabulary words from the Word Bank as possible in your writing.

Word Bank

apathetic	concerned	disenchanted	engaged
passionate	passive	zealous	

_____

_____

_____

_____

_____

_____

_____

_____

_____

_____

_____

_____

Condition of Material

Teacher Note

For detailed instructions on how to implement the components of this lesson, see pages 15–19.

Objective

Students will analyze words related to condition of material, from **less** to **more cared for**.

Materials

- *Vocabulary Ladders* template (page 142)
- *Activity Cards* (page 119)
- *Ordering Words* (page 120)
- *Sentence Clues* (page 121)
- *Sentence Stems* (page 122)
- *Write About It!* (page 123)

Additional Words

Introduce students to additional words such as *grimy, disheveled, orderly, pristine, immaculate,* and *clean* as you work through the lesson.

Answer Key

Vocabulary Ladders

Word	Definition
dilapidated	extremely shabby and falling apart
scraggly	very messy and ragged
dingy	dirty or faded
unkempt	messy and uncared for
well-kept	carefully looked after
tidy	especially neat and in order
spotless	perfectly clean

Ordering Words

Check that students can explain why the words are ordered the way they are.

Sentence Clues

1. Because she had a maid clean her house every other day, it was (well-kept/**spotless**).

2. Tony's well-worn shirt was old and (**dingy**/scraggly).

3. His room looked (**unkempt**) because there were toys all over the floor.

4. The kitchen was nice and (**tidy**) after all the dishes were washed and put away.

5. The (scraggly/**dilapidated**) building looked very unsafe to work in.

Sentence Stems

Check that student responses reflect the meaning of the underlined word in each sentence frame.

Write About It!

Check that responses include the new vocabulary terms used in the correct way.

Name: _____ Date: _____

Activity Cards

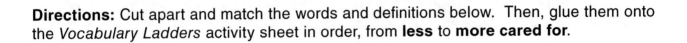

Directions: Cut apart and match the words and definitions below. Then, glue them onto the *Vocabulary Ladders* activity sheet in order, from **less** to **more cared for**.

dilapidated	perfectly clean
dingy	carefully looked after
scraggly	especially neat and in order
spotless	messy and uncared for
tidy	dirty or faded
unkempt	very messy and ragged
well-kept	extremely shabby and falling apart

Name: _____   Date: _____

Ordering Words

Directions: Write the words from the Word Bank in the order you choose, from **less** to **more cared for**, on the ladder. Then, explain why you put them in the order you chose.

Word Bank			
dilapidated	dingy	scraggly	spotless
tidy	unkempt	well-kept	

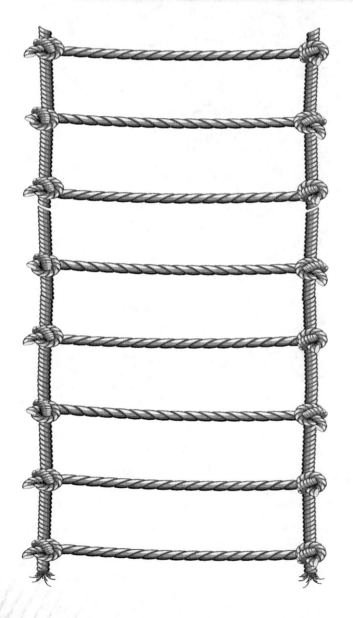

Explain why you ordered the words the way you did. You may use example sentences to help explain your thinking.

_____

_____

_____

_____

_____

_____

_____

_____

_____

_____

Name: _____ Date: _____

Sentence Clues

Directions: Choose the best word from the Word Bank to complete each sentence.
Note: You may need to add or change the ending of a word to make it fit the sentence.

Word Bank

| dilapidated | dingy | scraggly | spotless |
| tidy | unkempt | well-kept | |

1. Because she had a maid clean her house every other day, it was

   _____.

2. Tony's well-worn shirt was old and _____.

3. His room looked _____ because there were toys all

   over the floor.

4. The kitchen was nice and _____ after all the dishes

   were washed and put away.

5. The _____ building looked very unsafe to work in.

Directions: Create a fill-in-the-blank sentence on a separate sheet of paper for at least one of the words in this lesson. Use the sentences in the activity above as examples. Notice how a part of each sentence provides a clue about which word fits best. Have a partner fill in the missing word. Then, discuss why that word works best.

Name: _____ Date: _____

Sentence Stems

Directions: Complete each statement.

1. My bedroom is only <u>spotless</u> when _____

   _____

   _____ .

2. Mom and Dad are sure to <u>tidy</u> up our living room when _____

   _____

   _____ .

3. If I saw a <u>scraggly</u> looking dog I would feel _____

   _____

   _____ .

4. Our teacher makes sure our classroom is <u>well-kept</u> because _____

   _____

   _____ .

5. An <u>unkempt</u> house would make me feel _____

   _____

   _____ .

Name: _____   Date: _____

Write About It!

Directions: Read the prompt. Then, write a response. Underline the new vocabulary words you use in your response.

Compare and contrast the cleanliness of your bedroom to your parents' room. Try to use as many of your new vocabulary words from the Word Bank as possible in your writing.

Word Bank

dilapidated	dingy	scraggly
spotless	tidy	unkempt	well-kept

Pride

Teacher Note

For detailed instructions on how to implement the components of this lesson, see pages 15–19.

Objective

Students will analyze words related to pride, from **modest** to **proud**.

Materials

- *Vocabulary Ladders* template (page 142)
- *Activity Cards* (page 125)
- *Ordering Words* (page 126)
- *Sentence Clues* (page 127)
- *Sentence Stems* (page 128)
- *Write About It!* (page 129)

Additional Words

Introduce students to additional words such as *arrogant, proud, modest,* and *unassuming* as you work through the lesson.

Answer Key

Vocabulary Ladders

Word	Definition
humble	modest; not proud or arrogant
demure	quiet, shy, or reserved in manner
unpretentious	not displaying signs of wealth or high rank
smug	confident with oneself to the point of annoying other people
haughty	thinking of others as beneath oneself
pompous	showing an exaggerated air of importance
egotistical	excessively self-promoting

Ordering Words

Check that students can explain why the words are ordered the way they are.

Sentence Clues

1. His (smug) attitude made people not like him because they found it annoying.

2. The (haughty/smug) girl thinks she's better than everyone else.

3. No one liked the (pompous/egotistical) actor because he kept talking about himself.

4. On Kayla's first day at the new school, she seemed (demure), but kind.

5. That philanthropist is (unpretentious/humble) and generous even though he is famous and rich.

Sentence Stems

Check that student responses reflect the meaning of the underlined word in each sentence frame.

Write About It!

Check that responses include the new vocabulary terms used in the correct way.

Name: _____ Date: _____

Activity Cards

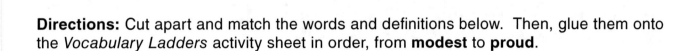

Directions: Cut apart and match the words and definitions below. Then, glue them onto the *Vocabulary Ladders* activity sheet in order, from **modest** to **proud**.

demure	excessively self-promoting
egotistical	showing an exaggerated air of importance
haughty	thinking of others as beneath oneself
humble	confident with oneself to the point of annoying other people
pompous	quiet, shy, or reserved in manner
smug	not displaying signs of wealth or high rank
unpretentious	modest; not proud or arrogant

Name: _____   Date: _____

Ordering Words

Directions: Write the words from the Word Bank in the order you choose, from **modest** to **proud**, on the ladder. Then, explain why you put them in the order you chose.

Word Bank

demure	egotistical	haughty	humble
pompous	smug	unpretentious	

Explain why you ordered the words the way you did. You may use example sentences to help explain your thinking.

_____

_____

_____

_____

_____

_____

_____

_____

_____

_____

Name: _____   Date: _____

Sentence Clues

Directions: Choose the best word from the Word Bank to complete each sentence.
Note: You may need to add or change the ending of a word to make it fit the sentence.

Word Bank

demure	egotistical	haughty	humble
pompous	smug	unpretentious	

---

1. His _____ attitude made people not like him because

   they found it annoying.

2. The _____ girl thinks she's better than everyone else.

3. No one liked the _____ actor because he kept talking

   about himself.

4. On Kayla's first day at the new school, she seemed

   _____, but kind.

5. That philanthropist is _____ and generous even

   though he is famous and rich.

Directions: Create a fill-in-the-blank sentence on a separate sheet of
paper for at least one of the words in this lesson. Use the sentences
in the activity above as examples. Notice how a part of each sentence
provides a clue about which word fits best. Have a partner fill in the
missing word. Then, discuss why that word works best.

Name: _____ Date: _____

Sentence Stems

Directions: Complete each statement.

1. I saw an actor behave <u>smugly</u> when _____

   _____

   _____.

2. I think people come across as <u>haughty</u> when _____

   _____

   _____.

3. It's hard to be <u>humble</u> when _____

   _____

   _____.

4. A rock star might be <u>pompous</u> if _____

   _____

   _____.

5. My uncle says that it's good to look <u>unpretentious</u> when _____

   _____

   _____.

 #51305—*Vocabulary Ladders: Understanding Word Nuances*

Name: _____ Date: _____

Write About It!

Directions: Read the prompt. Then, write a response. Underline the new vocabulary words you use in your response.

> Your best friend was elected class president. Write a story about how he or she reacted to the news. Try to use as many of your new vocabulary words from the Word Bank as possible in your writing.

Word Bank

demure	egotistical	haughty	humble
pompous	smug	unpretentious	

_____

_____

_____

_____

_____

_____

_____

_____

_____

_____

_____

_____

_____

Produce

Teacher Note

For detailed instructions on how to implement the components of this lesson, see pages 15–19.

Objective

Students will analyze words related to production, from **destroy** to **construct**.

Materials

- *Vocabulary Ladders* template (page 142)

- *Activity Cards* (page 131)

- *Ordering Words* (page 132)

- *Sentence Clues* (page 133)

- *Sentence Stems* (page 134)

- *Write About It!* (page 135)

Additional Words

Introduce students to additional words such as *obliterate, exterminate, construct, repair, spawn,* and *wipe out* as you work through the lesson.

Answer Key

Vocabulary Ladders

Word	Definition
annihilate	to destroy completely; to reduce to nothing
eradicate	to get rid of something completely
decimate	to destroy large portions of something
restore	to return to original condition
assemble	to put or collect components together
create	to make or design something new
generate	to bring into existence

Ordering Words

Check that students can explain why the words are ordered the way they are.

Sentence Clues

1. It is difficult for some artists to (create/generate) new ideas for songs.

2. I patiently watched my dad (assemble) my new bike this afternoon.

3. It took a few years to (restore) the old football stadium.

4. The engulfing flames from the fire (eradicated/annihilated) the top floor of our house in minutes.

5. After the dust settled, Kent realized he had (decimated) part of his garage door when he ran into it with his rideable lawn mower.

Sentence Stems

Check that student responses reflect the meaning of the underlined word in each sentence frame.

Write About It!

Check that responses include the new vocabulary terms used in the correct way.

Name: _____ Date: _____

Activity Cards

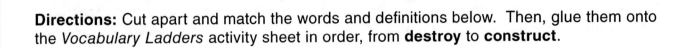

Directions: Cut apart and match the words and definitions below. Then, glue them onto the *Vocabulary Ladders* activity sheet in order, from **destroy** to **construct**.

annihilate	to bring into existence
assemble	to make or design something new
create	to put or collect components together
decimate	to return to original condition
eradicate	to destroy large portions of something
generate	to get rid of something completely
restore	to destroy completely; to reduce to nothing

Name: _____ Date: _____

Ordering Words

Directions: Write the words from the Word Bank in the order you choose, from **destroy** to **construct**, on the ladder. Then, explain why you put them in the order you chose.

Word Bank			
annihilate	assemble	create	decimate
eradicate	generate	restore	

Explain why you ordered the words the way you did. You may use example sentences to help explain your thinking.

_____

_____

_____

_____

_____

_____

_____

_____

_____

_____

Name: _____ Date: _____

Sentence Clues

Directions: Choose the best word from the Word Bank to complete each sentence.
Note: You may need to add or change the ending of a word to make it fit the sentence.

Word Bank

annihilate   assemble   create   decimate

eradicate   generate   restore

---

1. It is difficult for some artists to _____ new ideas for songs.

2. I patiently watched my dad _____ my new bike this afternoon.

3. It took a few years to _____ the old football stadium.

4. The engulfing flames from the fire _____ the top floor of our house in minutes.

5. After the dust settled, Kent realized he had _____ part of his garage door when he ran into it with his rideable lawn mower.

Directions: Create a fill-in-the-blank sentence on a separate sheet of paper for at least one of the words in this lesson. Use the sentences in the activity above as examples. Notice how a part of each sentence provides a clue about which word fits best. Have a partner fill in the missing word. Then, discuss why that word works best.

Name: _____   Date: _____

Sentence Stems

Directions: Complete each statement.

1. All the students in my school <u>assembled</u> in the gym when _____

   _____

   _____ .

2. A ship might be <u>annihilated</u> if _____

   _____

   _____ .

3. After an argument with my friend, I decided to <u>restore</u> the friendship by

   _____

   _____ .

4. The invading army <u>decimated</u> the enemy by _____

   _____

   _____ .

5. I <u>generate</u> my best ideas when _____

   _____

   _____ .

Name: _____ Date: _____

Write About It!

Directions: Read the prompt. Then, write a response. Underline the new vocabulary words you use in your response.

Imagine that you are caught in the middle of a horrible storm. Describe what you see, hear, and smell. Try to use as many of your new vocabulary words from the Word Bank as possible in your writing.

Word Bank

annihilate	assemble	create	decimate
eradicate	generate	restore	

_____

_____

_____

_____

_____

_____

_____

_____

_____

_____

_____

_____

Taking and Giving

Teacher Note

For detailed instructions on how to implement the components of this lesson, see pages 15–19.

Objective

Students will analyze words related to taking and giving, from **take** to **give**.

Materials

- *Vocabulary Ladders* template (page 142)

- *Activity Cards* (page 137)

- *Ordering Words* (page 138)

- *Sentence Clues* (page 139)

- *Sentence Stems* (page 140)

- *Write About It!* (page 141)

Additional Words

Introduce students to additional words such as *bestow, award, pilfer, embezzle, give,* and *provide* as you work through the lesson.

Answer Key

Vocabulary Ladders

Word	Definition
steal	to take something without permission
confiscate	to take something away as punishment
borrow	to use somebody else's property with their permission
transfer	to move from one place to another
contribute	to donate money or time
supply	to provide; satisfy a need or want
grant	to allow something as a favor

Ordering Words

Check that students can explain why the words are ordered the way they are.

Sentence Clues

1. My mom needed to (transfer) money from her savings account to her checking account this morning in order to pay a bill.

2. I want to (borrow) my best friend's new jacket, but I'm not sure how to ask her.

3. It was necessary for my parents to (grant) their permission for me to go on the field trip.

4. The organization (supplies/contributes) food for soldiers overseas.

5. When you (steal) from a store, you will get in trouble with the police.

Sentence Stems

Check that student responses reflect the meaning of the underlined word in each sentence frame.

Write About It!

Check that responses include the new vocabulary terms used in the correct way.

Name: _____ Date: _____

Activity Cards

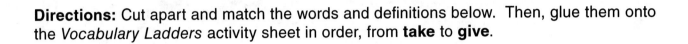

Directions: Cut apart and match the words and definitions below. Then, glue them onto the *Vocabulary Ladders* activity sheet in order, from **take** to **give**.

borrow	to allow something as a favor
confiscate	to provide; satisfy a need or want
contribute	to donate money or time
grant	to move from one place to another
steal	to use somebody else's property with their permission
supply	to take something away as punishment
transfer	to take something without permission

Name: _____   Date: _____

Ordering Words

Directions: Write the words from the Word Bank in the order you choose, from **take** to **give**, on the ladder. Then, explain why you put them in the order you chose.

Word Bank

borrow	confiscate	contribute	grant
steal	supply	transfer	

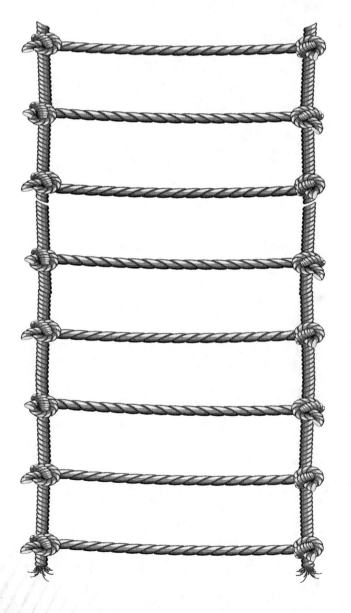

Explain why you ordered the words the way you did. You may use example sentences to help explain your thinking.

_____

_____

_____

_____

_____

_____

_____

_____

_____

_____

_____

Name: _____ Date: _____

Sentence Clues

Directions: Choose the best word from the Word Bank to complete each sentence.
Note: You may need to add or change the ending of a word to make it fit the sentence.

Word Bank

borrow	confiscate	contribute	grant
steal	supply	transfer	

---

1. My mom needed to _____ money from her savings account to her checking account this morning in order to pay a bill.

2. I want to _____ my best friend's new jacket, but I'm not sure how to ask her.

3. It was necessary for my parents to _____ their permission for me to go on the field trip.

4. The organization _____ food for soldiers overseas.

5. When you _____ from a store, you will get in trouble with the police.

Directions: Create a fill-in-the-blank sentence on a separate sheet of paper for at least one of the words in this lesson. Use the sentences in the activity above as examples. Notice how a part of each sentence provides a clue about which word fits best. Have a partner fill in the missing word. Then, discuss why that word works best.

Name: _____ Date: _____

Sentence Stems

Directions: Complete each statement.

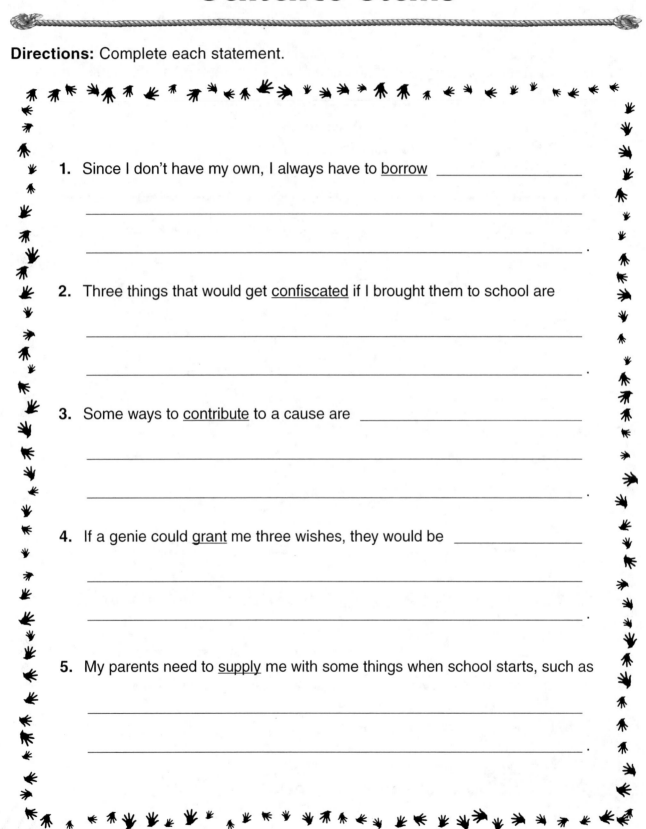

1. Since I don't have my own, I always have to <u>borrow</u> _____

   _____

   _____ .

2. Three things that would get <u>confiscated</u> if I brought them to school are

   _____

   _____ .

3. Some ways to <u>contribute</u> to a cause are _____

   _____

   _____ .

4. If a genie could <u>grant</u> me three wishes, they would be _____

   _____

   _____ .

5. My parents need to <u>supply</u> me with some things when school starts, such as

   _____

   _____ .

Name: _____ Date: _____

Write About It!

Directions: Read the prompt. Then, write a response. Underline the new vocabulary words you use in your response.

Imagine that you won a million dollars. Describe what you would do with the money. Try to use as many of your new vocabulary words from the Word Bank as possible in your writing.

Word Bank

borrow	confiscate	contribute	
grant	steal	supply	transfer

_____

_____

_____

_____

_____

_____

_____

_____

_____

_____

_____

_____

_____

Vocabulary Ladders

Directions: Match the cut out words and definitions. Then, glue them in the correct order on the ladders.

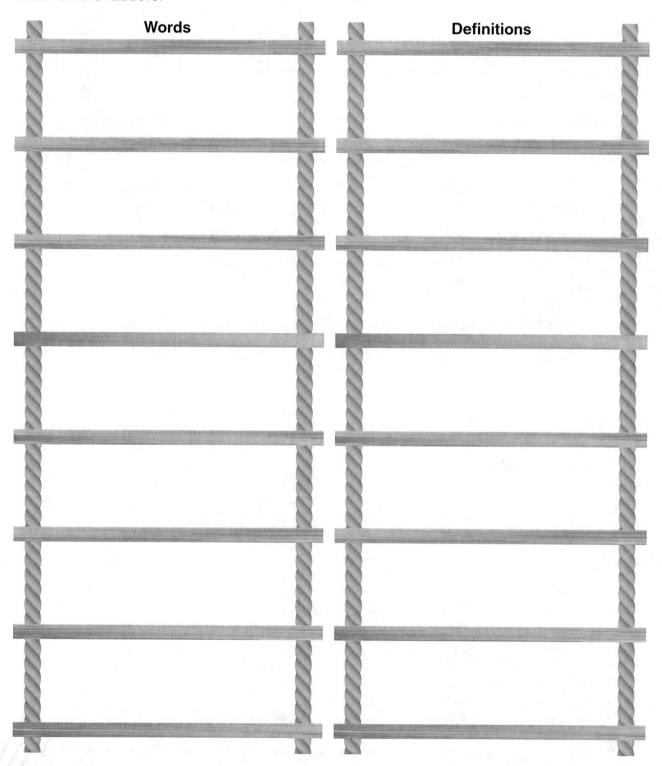

Words

Definitions

References Cited

Anderson, Richard. C., and Peter Freebody. 1981. "Vocabulary Knowledge." In *Comprehension and Teaching: Research Reviews,* edited by John T. Guthrie, 77–117. Newark, DE: International Reading Association.

———. 1983. "Reading Comprehension and the Assessment and Acquisition of Word Knowledge." In *Advances in Reading/Language Research*, edited by Barbara A. Hutson, 231–256. Greenwich, CT: JAI Press.

Becker, Wesley C. 1977. "Teaching Reading and Language to the Disadvantaged: What We Have Learned from Field Research." *Harvard Educational Review* 47: 518–543.

Brabham, Edna, Connie Bukist, Coman Henderson, Timon Paleologos, and Nikki Baugh. 2012. "Flooding Vocabulary Gaps to Accelerate Word Learning." *The Reading Teacher* 65: 523–533.

Davis, Frederick. 1944. "Fundamental Factors in Reading Comprehension." *Psychometrika* 9: 185–197.

Nagy, William. 1988. "Teaching Vocabulary to Improve Teading Comprehension." Newark, DE: International Reading Association.

National Reading Panel. 2000. "Report of the National Reading Panel: Teaching Children to Read: An Evidence-Based Assessment of Scientific Research Literature on Reading and Its Implications for Instruction: Report of the Subgroups." Washington, DC: US Department of Health and Human Services.

Rasinski, Timothy and Jerry Zutell. 2010. *Essential Strategies for Word Study: Effective Methods for Improving Decoding, Spelling, and Vocabulary.* New York: Scholastic.

Stahl, Steve. 1986. "Three Principles of Effective Vocabulary Instruction." *Journal of Reading* 29: 662–668.

Contents of the Digital Resource CD

Lessons

Pages	Lesson	Filename
22–27	Spending Money	spendingmoney.pdf
28–33	How Something Sounds: Loudness	loudness.pdf
34–39	Tastiness	tastiness.pdf
40–45	Amount of Something	amountofsomething.pdf
46–51	Range of Emotion	rangeofemotion.pdf
52–57	To Ask	toask.pdf
58–63	Likeability	likeability.pdf
64–69	Said: Emotion	saidemotion.pdf
70–75	Move and Carry	moveandcarry.pdf
76–81	Direction of Travel	directionoftravel.pdf
82–87	Moving Forward	movingforward.pdf
88–93	Personal Attitude or Appearance	attitudeorappearance.pdf
94–99	Level of Difficulty in Work	levelofdifficulty.pdf
100–105	Level of Interest	levelofinterest.pdf
106–111	Entertainment	entertainment.pdf
112–117	Showing Interest	showinginterest.pdf
118–123	Condition of Material	conditionofmaterial.pdf
124–129	Pride	pride.pdf
130–135	Produce	produce.pdf
136–141	Taking and Giving	takingandgiving.pdf

Additional Resources

Page	Resource	Filename
21	Standards Chart	standards.pdf
142	Vocabulary Ladders	vocabularyladders.pdf
NA	Additional Lessons	additionallessons.pdf
NA	Activity Cards Template	cardstemplate.pdf
NA	WORDO	wordo.pdf